How to Stop Yelling

—(A Peaceful Parenting Guide)—

7 Days Challenge to Control Stress, Anger Management,
and Learn Emotional Strategies: Practical Tips for
Family Harmony, and Positive Discipline.

By Rebecca Elwin

Table of Contents

Why I Write This Book and 6

What to Expect from it !...6

Let's Start ! 13

Chapter 1: Let's Understand Why You Feel Stuck

Are you sick of always yelling? Let's find out why. 20

What's really causing your stress as a parent? 26

How Your Brain Reacts Under Pressure...33

Chapter 2: Take Charge of Your Emotions

Frustrated? Here's How to Stay Grounded in the Moment. 44

Learn how your anger affects your child and break the cycle............50

Turn Reactivity into Calm: Your Path to a Peaceful Mindset............57

Chapter 3: Build Stronger Connections with Your Family

Stop the Conflict. 68

Do you want more trust and love in your home? Let's build it..........74

How to stay calm and in control when it matters most....................80

Chapter 4: Take Care of Yourself and Grow Together

Feeling drained? Here's How to Reclaim Your Energy. 90

Struggling to stop yelling? Let's Break That Habit Now!...................96

You're Stronger Than You Think: Find Your Inner Power...............102

Chapter 5: Create a Home Filled with Respect and Harmony

Want your child to respect you? Here's how.............112

Discipline Without Fear...118

Raise resilient children and form stronger families together. ..125

Chapter 6: Tackle Everyday Challenges with Confidence

Challenge Day One 136

Challenge Day 2...143

Challenge Day 3...150

Challenge Day 4...156

Challenge Day 5:..163

Challenge Day 6...169

Challenge Day 7 175

Conclusion. 181

Aknowledgments 186

Resources..188

Free Gift...190

This book is dedicated to every parent who has ever experienced feelings of overwhelm, frustration, or uncertainty. This book is for you, because you deserve a serene house, a calm heart, and a strong, loving relationship with your children. May this journey help you rediscover your feeling of calm and joy in the most essential role of all: parenthood. With love and thanks,

Rebecca Elwin

Why I Write This Book and What to Expect from It !

Parenting is one of the most gratifying and stressful experiences someone can have. As parents, we want to provide a supportive, loving atmosphere in which our children may feel secure, heard, and understood. However, the stresses of daily life, including managing work, obligations, and our children's needs, overwhelm many of us. Over time, these pressures might cause dissatisfaction, rage, and, in some cases, yelling. Overwhelmed, upset, or unsure how to handle the pressure, we shout.

I know this because I have been there. I, too, once felt imprisoned in a cycle of wrath and frustration. I wanted to be the calm, patient parent I envisaged, but I frequently lost control, raised my voice, and felt awful afterwards. I was desperate for a solution that would allow me to better regulate my emotions and interact with my children. But every answer I saw seemed either too intricate, too unclear, or just didn't fit into the realities of my hectic lifestyle.

That is why I wrote the book. I wanted to build something that was approachable, practical, and grounded in reality. This is not another parenting book that instructs you to "just relax" or "breathe deeply" in the heat of the moment. This book is for parents who have tried everything yet still struggle to manage their anger and stress. It's for parents who are feeling stuck, don't know where to turn, and want to make a difference but need a little help getting there.

My personal parenting experiences inspired this book. What I noticed was missing was a step-by-step strategy that not only addressed the emotional issues of parenting but also offered practical, tangible tactics for building a tranquil household. As I began reading, learning, and trying various ways, I realized that having a tranquil and balanced house did not require perfection or one-size-fits-all guidance. It was about first learning how to control my own emotions, then identifying the triggers that caused tension and anger, and lastly finding practical measures to promote family peace.

The next pages provide a simple, easy-to-follow 7-day challenge meant to help you get control of your emotions and quit screaming. I understand how simple it is to get into a cycle of worry and frustration, but I also believe that change is possible. The strategies I'll share with you have benefited me, and I believe they can assist you as well. This book explains why you feel stuck and gives you the skills to break free from that loop.

We designed the 7-day challenge to allow you to start slowly and gradually increase your progress each day. Whether you're struggling with anger management, exhausted by the demands of daily life, or simply want to create a more peaceful environment at home, this book will help you understand how your brain reacts under pressure and provide you with practical strategies for managing your emotions in real time. You'll discover how to stay grounded in times of irritation, how to communicate effectively with your children, and how to build a stronger, more loving bond with them.

I understand that as a parent, it might feel like you are continuously giving without ever having time for yourself. However, it's crucial to realize that self-care isn't selfish; it's necessary. When you take care of your own mental and emotional health, you'll be better prepared to face the challenges that come with parenting. An important lesson I've learned from this journey is that self-care benefits you and your children. Fill your cup with serenity, love, and self-compassion because you can't pour from an empty one.

The central theme of this book is to break away from the destructive cycle of anger and frustration and instead create a household filled with respect, trust, and love. It is about establishing an environment in which communication flows easily, discipline is based on understanding, and both parents and children thrive. Parenting does not have to include continual strife or feelings of failure. It could involve creating something beautiful and lasting with your family that will benefit you for years.

Throughout this book, you'll find a variety of tools and tactics to help you regulate your emotions, stop the yelling habit, and build greater relationships with your kids. From self-care techniques to parenting advice, this book will walk you through each stage of the process, giving you the confidence and clarity you need to establish a harmonious household. I'll lead you through the fundamentals of emotional intelligence, anger management methods, and practical strategies for connecting with your children on a deeper level.

You'll also get real-world examples, activities, and reflections to help you apply what you've learned. It's not about perfection but about making tiny, practical moves that will lead to huge improvements in the long run. After reading this book, you'll have the tools to create a peaceful parenting style that works for you and your family.

Parenting, for me, is about connection. It is about educating our children via our deeds as much as our words. If we can learn to regulate our emotions, be present for our children in the most important moments, and foster a tranquil environment, we will be giving them the greatest gift we can. We're teaching kids how to manage their emotions, how to handle disagreement gracefully, and how to face the world with love and respect.

Maya Angelou eloquently put it: "We all should know that diversity makes for a rich tapestry, and we must understand that all the threads of the tapestry are equal in value no matter their color." Parenting is no different. Every child is different, and each parent has their own path. Even right now, you can bring peace and harmony to your home. It's never too late to start, and you're not alone.

This book is my present to you—a handbook that I hope will inspire and motivate you to approach your position as a parent with confidence, clarity, and love. Let's end the cycle of tension and anger and build the calm home you and your family deserve.

INTRODUCTION

"The boundary to what we can accept is the boundary to our freedom." - N. Scott Momaday

Let's Start !

Parenting is difficult. I do not need to tell you that. You already know. It is taxing, emotional, and, at times, completely overpowering. No matter how much you love your children or how much you want the best for them, there are times when it all feels overwhelming. As our stress levels increase and our patience diminishes, we resort to what we had vowed not to do: we yell.

If you've ever found yourself raising your voice at your child, feeling awful afterwards, and vowing to do better next time, you're not alone. Many parents become stuck in this pattern. When the pressure mounts, yelling seems like the easiest approach, but we all know it isn't. We aspire to be the calm, patient parents who respond with understanding and grace. But how?

That's precisely why I wrote this book. I have been where you are. I've felt the sting of fury in my chest, remorse in my heart, and hopelessness in my head. I've been that parent, standing in the middle of a tumultuous scenario, thinking I could simply take a big breath, relax, and approach things differently. And for a long time, I was unsure how to break the loop. I wasn't sure how to quit shouting.

However, I have resolved the issue and would like to share it with you.

Parents who are tired of feeling out of control should read this book. It is for parents who seek more than a quick cure or hollow counsel. It's for individuals who want to change and are sick of the shouting, worry, guilt, and anger. If you aspire to establish a peaceful home where love, respect, and understanding serve as the foundation of your family's relationships, this program is for you.

I recognize that the advice I will provide is not universally applicable. Parenting is an inherently personal experience. It is unique to each family and fraught with complexity. But the one element that unites all of us as parents is our desire to do our best for our children. We aim to provide a home setting in which kids feel loved, supported, and protected. The problem is figuring out how to deal with stress, disagreement, and difficult periods when everything seems to be falling apart.

That is where this book comes in.

In these pages, I'll walk you through a simple but

effective 7-day challenge to help you get control of your emotions, regulate your anger, and establish a tranquil, loving household. This isn't merely an abstract concept or a comprehensive list of actions to take during moments of calm and relaxation. This is a plan for actual, daily life—the type of life when stress is unavoidable, irritation is common, and things don't always go as planned.

To handle such moments gracefully and calmly, you must understand how your emotions work and how to respond in a way that supports you and your child. That's what this book will assist you with. We'll look at ways to identify stressors, regulate those emotions in real time, and lay the groundwork for long-term family harmony.

The 7-day challenge focuses on progress rather than perfection. Every day, you will take small steps that will result in significant improvements. These are neither unachievable tasks nor unreasonable aspirations. These are practical, concrete measures that you may include in your daily life. These ideas can assist you whether you're a working parent managing a busy schedule, a stay-at-home parent managing constant requests, or someone who is simply trying to figure everything out.

You do not need to be flawless. In reality, the aim is not perfection. The objective is to be present and thoughtful and learn to manage your emotions in a way that promotes understanding and connection with your children. This is the actual power of calm parenting.

But let me be clear: this is not going to be easy. Change never occurs. It takes work, patience, and a desire to attempt something new. Sometimes it seems like nothing is working, you want to give up, or you want to shout. That is okay. What matters is that you persevere. Because every time you choose to remain calm, listen, and respond instead of react, you are making progress in regulating your emotions.

Imagine a household without shouting as a stress response. Consider a family where talks flow rather than fights. Imagine a home where you and your kids can collaborate to resolve issues, fostering mutual understanding and respect, instead of escalating into conflict and fury. That is what I want for you. That's what I think is doable.

The 7-day challenge will help you get there. It is not necessary to cure everything all at once; rather, tiny, meaningful modifications can lead to significant benefits. Each day builds on the previous one, so by the end of the week, you'll have a better awareness of your emotional triggers, more ways to calm yourself in the present, and a stronger bond with your children.

But here's the truth: this book is about more than simply not yelling. It's about changing your mentality, your conduct, and how you approach parenting. Learning to manage stress without compromising your health or family's happiness is key. It is about producing long-term change, not only for today or tomorrow.

As you go through this process, realize one thing: you are not alone. Every parent feels overwhelmed. Every parent struggles. But every parent has the ability to evolve, develop, and establish the type of family dynamic they want. You are capable of making this transition, and I am here to help you every step of the way.

So, are they ready to quit yelling and begin establishing the quiet, loving home they've always desired? If yes, let us begin. The route to a more peaceful, fulfilling parenting experience begins here. Take one step at a time. Together.

Chapter 1: Let's Understand Why You Feel Stuck

"Stress is not something we experience. It is our response to what occurs. We have the ability to choose the answer. — Maureen Killoran

ARE YOU SICK OF ALWAYS YELLING? LET'S FIND OUT WHY.

You've been there, correct? When your tolerance reaches its limit, you find yourself unable to refrain from expressing yourself loudly and angrily. You've promised yourself a hundred times that today will be different, that you will not shout. But somehow you're back in the same loop. The frustration mounts, and you once again lose control.

It is exhausting. It is overpowering. If you're anything like most parents, you probably feel horrible afterwards, wishing you could take it all back. You notice the same worry creeping in throughout the day. The cycle repeats. You convince yourself you'll do better next time, but that doesn't always happen.

You are not alone in your fight. In truth, numerous parents are right alongside you, attempting to combine the obligations of raising children with the realities of life's obstacles. And the truth is, the reason you continue to shout is not because you are a negligent parent or lack concern. It's because something deeper is going on—something you may not even be aware of.

So let's take a step back and look at why this continues happening. Breaking free from the loop of shouting begins with understanding why it's happening. Most importantly, we'll learn what's happening behind the scenes and how to change it.

<u>Why do we yell?</u>

Let's start with the basics: why are you yelling in the first place? It's tempting to assume it's because your youngster isn't listening or has pushed you too far. Indeed, that may be the case at the moment. However, the larger picture is that shouting is frequently a stress reaction rather than a child's conduct. In reality, it is more about your mental condition than your child's actions.

Consider this: when you're feeling overwhelmed, frustrated, or anxious, your capacity to control your emotions reduces. Your patience wanes. When you reach your breaking point, your brain goes to the fastest, simplest approach to seek attention or vent your frustration: shouting. It's not about intending to harm your child; it's about attempting to regain control of a situation that feels out of hand.

Think about the last time you screamed. Were you already stressed from work, exhausted after a long day, or coping with something other than your parenting role?

These external factors—the pressures you face on a daily basis—have a significant impact on how you behave in times of parental stress. Your mind and body are already on edge, and when you feel like you can't handle one more thing, the stress typically spills over.

So it's not simply your child's conduct that is causing your outbursts. It represents all that is happening on the inside of you. The accumulation of all the minor details—stress, tiredness, and self-doubt—can make a calm response appear unattainable.

The Emotional Toll of Parenting

Parenting is not only physically hard, but also emotionally draining. No one can prepare you for the emotional toll of parenthood—the continual concern, the mental juggling, the dread of not being sufficient. Add that emotional burden to an already hectic day, and it's no surprise that your patience becomes frayed.

Have you ever noticed how, when you're emotionally exhausted, even the simplest things may set you off? Maybe your child's loud voice seems a hundred decibels too high. Or maybe a cluttered space leaves you stressed out, even if you've told yourself a million times it's not a big problem. It's in these moments that the weight of everything becomes overpowering, and shouting becomes a means to relieve the strain.

The fact is that you cannot pour from an empty cup. When you exhaust your emotional energy, it becomes more challenging to respond calmly and with empathy. When you're feeling exhausted, you may lash out or feel alienated from your child, which adds to your guilt and anger.

But here's the positive news: Recognizing that your emotions are controlling your behavior is the first step toward recovering your authority. It's not about blaming yourself for shouting; it's about understanding that your emotional state has a significant impact on how you connect with your child. Recognizing this allows you to start changing your reactions and, eventually, your parenting style.

What Happens to Our Brain During Stress?

It is one thing to recognize that emotions have a role in screaming. But what happens in your brain when you cross the threshold?

When you are under stress, your brain initiates the "fight or flight" reaction. This is a survival system that developed to keep us safe in perilous conditions. The challenge lies in the fact that we don't always face life-threatening situations in our modern lives. Nonetheless, our brain reacts in the same manner to daily stressors such as a screaming newborn, a disorganized house, or a youngster who refuses to follow directions.

When this occurs, your brain secretes stress chemicals such as cortisol and adrenaline, preparing your body to react swiftly. Your heart rate rises, your breathing gets shallow, and your body prepares for action. However, during these moments, your rational thinking—the ability to pause, reflect, and make a sound decision—turns off.

Instead of responding calmly, your brain switches to reactive mode. As if a switch flips, you find yourself compelled to react, often in ways you'll later regret. That's why, even when you know shouting isn't the solution, it feels like you can't stop yourself in the moment.

"The best way to predict your future is to create it." This statement by Abraham Lincoln emphasizes the importance of intentionality. The future you desire as a parent, a quiet and tranquil one, does not come by chance. Creating the gap between stimuli and reaction requires mindfulness and awareness—the capacity to pause and choose how to react rather than allowing your emotions to dictate your actions.

The Guilt Cycle: Why It's Difficult to Change

After the shouting comes guilt. You relive the situation in your head, wishing you had handled it differently. Perhaps you experience feelings of failure or doubt your suitability for parenthood. The shame is overwhelming, and it frequently drives further stress, making it much more difficult to stop the pattern.

But here's the truth: feeling guilty makes nothing better. It does not improve the problem or make you a better parent. In many cases, it exacerbates the situation. Guilt can increase tension, which leads to increased emotional outbursts, including screaming. It's a terrible cycle, and if you don't intervene, you'll quickly find yourself trapped.

Instead of dwelling on guilt, I want you to consider why it happens. Guilt is an emotional response that indicates a misalignment between your acts and your principles. You want to be a calm, caring parent, yet your actions in stressful situations contradict that wish. But this does not make you a negligent parent; rather, it makes you a human one.

Self-compassion is the key to overcoming the cycle of guilt. Understand that parenting is difficult, and you will make errors. But each day presents a fresh opportunity to improve, learn, and develop. Don't allow guilt to hold you back; instead, use it to motivate yourself and your family to make better decisions.

What can you do?

If you're weary of shouting and want to stop the pattern, it's time to make a change. Begin by identifying the underlying reasons for your stress and emotions. Take a step back and consider the external demands in your life. Are there any particular triggers—work, lack of sleep, personal challenges—that add to your stress levels?

Once you've identified the stressors, the next step is to develop strategies to manage them effectively. Practice mindfulness and emotional control so that when stress strikes, you have tools to remain calm. Begin small and commit to taking a breath before reacting. With practice, it gets easier to respond patiently and understandably.

And remember that this is a journey, not a sprint. It is OK to make mistakes sometimes. Your determination to improve and take responsibility for your emotional health matters. You may create the tranquil, caring environment you wish.

What's really causing your stress as a parent?

Let's face it—parenting isn't easy. If it were, we wouldn't be having this discussion right now. You've undoubtedly felt it—constant pressure, never-ending tiredness, and an overpowering sensation that you're not doing enough. Sometimes it feels like you're going around with a weight on your shoulders, and every little thing feels like it may be the final straw.

But let's be honest for a moment: what's actually causing your stress as a parent? Is this your child's behavior? What's with the incessant clutter around the house? Do you find yourself accumulating endless tasks that never seem to finish? Is there a deeper issue at play, something you haven't fully acknowledged?

When you think about it, it's more than one thing. Many factors combine to create a confluence of stress and discontent. What is the positive news? Understanding what is creating this tension is the first step toward addressing it. Let's break it down together.

The Weight of Expectations: What You Believe You Should Be Doing

Consider the expectations you face as a parent. Do you feel their weight? There is a constant expectation to remain patient, caring, and in command. We anticipate maintaining order, tranquility, and perfect harmony in everything. There is constant pressure to embody the ideal of a "perfect parent," ensuring that every response, attitude, and tone of voice is consistently appropriate.

The reality is, no one can consistently match those standards. Falling short (as we all do) causes worry and frustration. You could start wondering, "Why can't I keep it together?" or "Why am I always yelling?"

This is a vicious cycle. As you doubt your ability to meet these high standards, your anxiety grows. That tension adds up, and when a difficult situation develops with your child, it becomes much more difficult to remain calm. And, inevitably, you shout. The cycle continues.

These unreasonable expectations affect not just you, but also your connection with your child. You may believe you are providing an example of discipline or responsibility, but your stress is teaching your child to constantly strive for perfection and never be vulnerable. However, it's important to acknowledge that no one, including yourself, can consistently achieve perfection, and that's a positive aspect. Accepting imperfection is the first step in stopping the cycle of stress.

Unseen Stressors: The Hidden Burden of Parenthood.

Now, let's discuss something frequently overlooked: the invisible strains of motherhood. These aren't the apparent stressors, such as a tantrum or a disorganized room. No, they are the silent, lingering pressures that eat away at your emotional resources.

Are you feeling overwhelmed by how much work you have to complete every day? Perhaps your to-do list seems never-ending, and the strain to juggle parenting with everything else is overwhelming. Perhaps financial problems, health concerns, or relationship issues are eating up your brain space and leaving you emotionally exhausted.

It's tempting to dismiss these concerns as unrelated to parenting, but the fact is that they influence your capacity to behave calmly in tough situations. When you have a mental load of worries and fears, it's far more difficult to be present with your child, much less respond to their needs with compassion and understanding.

Consider how much energy you devote to managing the mental burden of daily living. There's always something to remember: appointments, bills, and deadlines. Managing your to-do list and the emotional demands of parenting can drain your mental energy. These hidden stresses may not be visible to others, but they can affect your immediate behavior.

The Effects of Exhaustion: When Sleep Is Stranger

You are familiar with the sensation of waking up

exhausted, struggling to get through the day, and experiencing a sense of exhaustion. Lack of sleep is a key cause of stress, and many parents are all too familiar with it. Whether it's the demands of a baby, sleepless nights with a toddler, or late evenings trying to catch up on everything else in life, sleep deprivation may have a negative impact on your mental and emotional health.

Sleep deprivation impairs your brain's capacity to tolerate stress. When you're weary, the prefrontal cortex, the region of your brain responsible for emotion regulation, doesn't function properly. You are more inclined to snap, become overwhelmed, and respond out of frustration rather than calmness. Not only are you weary, but you're also under a lot of stress, which makes it difficult to control your emotions.

Not getting enough sleep brings guilt. You feel guilty for not being there for your child, for not having the energy to play, or for being perfect. That shame exacerbates your tension, producing a vicious cycle that is even more difficult to stop.

So, what can you do about this? The first step is to recognize the significance of sleep loss in your stress levels. Next, make self-care a priority, even if just in little ways. It might entail asking for help when you can, taking short naps, or finding strategies to sleep better at night. By controlling your sleep, you may start managing your stress more successfully.

The Struggle with Time: The Endless To-Do List

Time is a limited resource, and as a parent, it seems like

there is never enough of it. You have a hundred things to accomplish and just a fraction of the time to complete them. The pressure to do everything for everyone might make you feel overwhelmed and overworked.

This is especially true when it comes to managing your child's needs with everything else you have to do—work, housework, appointments, errands, and so on. It seems like there's always more to do, no matter how much you do. This persistent time pressure accumulates and leads directly to your stress.

The fight is genuine. There are no simple solutions to time management; the key is to discover ways to shift your focus. Rather than attempting to accomplish everything at once, divide work into manageable chunks and prioritize what is truly important. Recognizing that not everything requires precision or promptness may simplify the process. When you manage your time with intention, you will feel less overwhelmed, which will automatically lessen your stress.

<u>The Social Comparison Trap.</u>

Do you ever find yourself comparing your parenting to other people's? Perhaps you see a friend on social media boasting about their immaculately organized home, well-behaved children, and excellent work, and you can't help but feel inadequate. Social comparison often leads to feelings of inadequacy and shame, causing significant stress for many parents.

Social media can have both positive and negative effects in today's society. While it helps us connect with people, it may also lead to unreasonable expectations. We frequently see just the highlight reels—the beautiful moments—and forget that every Instagram post has genuine hardships and flawed moments. Comparing yourself to these chosen photos increases your tension and makes you feel like you're not accomplishing enough.

Remember that your parenting path is unique to you. It isn't about meeting someone else's expectations; it's about doing your best for your family in a way that is consistent with your principles. Don't let the strain of comparison make you stressed. Instead, concentrate on your own development and the progress you're making every day.

<u>Breaking Free of the Stress Cycle</u>

So, what do you do with all of this? First, recognize that a variety of interwoven factors cause your stress. By recognizing the main stresses in your life, you may start addressing them one at a time. Whether it's unreasonable expectations, hidden obligations, weariness, or time constraints, the first step is to recognize that these pressures exist and are acceptable.

Once you've identified what's causing your stress, you can start implementing techniques to decrease its impact. This might include establishing boundaries, seeking assistance, or shifting your perspective on perfection. Be kind to yourself—you're doing your best, and that's enough.

As Albert Einstein once remarked, "The ability to change is the measure of intelligence." The fact that you're here, reading this, indicates that you're open to change.

And that, my friend, is the first step toward a more pleasant and rewarding parenting experience. So, let us continue this journey together—step by step, day by day—to a calmer, more connected parenting style.

How Your Brain Reacts Under Pressure: What You Can Do

Let's discuss something most parents overlook: how your brain behaves under pressure. It's something we don't always completely grasp, but it has a significant impact on how we respond to stress, irritation, and even fury as parents.

Consider this: you've had a long day. You're balancing work, your child's demands, the shopping list, and an ever-growing to-do list. Suddenly, your child starts expressing distress over a seemingly insignificant issue. Perhaps they desire a toy but are unable to obtain it, or they refuse to eat supper. Everything seems to be falling apart at that point.

Your pulse rate rises, your fingers get clammy, and before you realize it, the familiar wave of rage and fury takes hold. You may shout, raise your voice, or become overwhelmed by the circumstance, wondering why you can't remain calm.

So, what's going through your mind right now? Why is it so difficult to respond in a calm, controlled manner when everything inside you is screaming for relief?

Let us break it down. Understanding the science underlying your emotions might help you manage these situations more effectively. So please bear with me. We'll dig deep, and I promise you'll understand why you feel the way you do and, more importantly, how to fix it.

<u>The stress response is your brain's default mode.</u>

Simply put, stress triggers your brain to enter "survival mode." Humans have naturally adapted to this biological reaction for thousands of years. Back when humans were hunter-gatherers, survival mode kept us safe from predators and harmful conditions. It enabled us to respond swiftly, run fast, and protect ourselves.

However, in the current day, "predators" are not usually corporeal. Stressful conditions such as parental issues, work pressures, financial strain, and relationship problems shape their behavior. When you experience certain stressors, your brain produces substances such as cortisol and adrenaline to prepare you for action. This "fight-or-flight" response is your brain's method of defending you, but in a world where the risks are more emotional than physical, it might backfire.

You're in a scenario where you need to calmly manage an issue, such as guiding your youngster through a tantrum. Instead, your brain has activated survival systems, and you are behaving as if the situation is critical.

You may question, "Why can't I just take a deep breath

and think this over?" Why am I acting as if this is life or death?

The solution lies in the brain's instinctive response to stress. When stress occurs, the brain frequently skips the rational, thinking part—the prefrontal cortex—and transfers control to the emotional area, the amygdala. The amygdala functions like your brain's alarm system, continually checking for hazards. When it detects a "danger," even something as seemingly trivial as a tantrum, it reacts immediately, which can result in shouting or snapping before your brain has a time to consider a more controlled response.

<u>The overwhelming sensation of being 'triggered.</u>

You've undoubtedly been in circumstances when, despite your best efforts, your patience wears out and you snap. In those instances, it's more than simply being "tired" or "frustrated"; there's a fundamental, neurological reason why you're feeling overwhelmed. This answer may be overwhelming, particularly if you have a deep-seated desire to approach things differently.

In these situations, it's straightforward to be harsh on oneself. Perhaps you believe I should have known better. Why can't I simply be patient? But this self-blame will not help. Instead, we should focus on understanding and managing the situation. You see, the brain is not always your enemy; instead, it is attempting to protect you. However, in the context of parenting, this inclination may lead to less-than-ideal behaviors.

Consider this scenario: you're driving a car, and a

warning light appears on the dashboard. The brain, like the warning light, indicates that something is awry. However, instead of carefully examining the issue, the brain immediately enters emergency mode. This is why you may feel out of control—your brain is reacting to stress in the same manner it has for thousands of years.

Why Your Brain Needs a 'Cool-Down' Period

This is the point at which things start to get interesting. Your brain does not stay in the "fight or flight" condition indefinitely. Once the stressor has passed, the body begins to relax. The problem is that in our modern, fast-paced lifestyles, we seldom give ourselves adequate time to relax. Instead, we're racing from one task to the next with no downtime, and our brain doesn't get a chance to reset.

The longer we stay in this heightened condition, the more difficult it gets to handle stress in the long run. You may think powering through these stressful times is best, but being on "high alert" may wear you out. Burnout, anxiety, and emotional tiredness become more prevalent at this point.

This is why taking pauses and allowing yourself time to relax is essential for your mental health. Like any machine, your brain needs time to reset, refuel, and recalibrate. You may not always have the option of taking a long break, but taking tiny breaks—such as pausing for a few seconds to breathe or practicing mindfulness—can help your brain return to a peaceful, balanced state. This does not imply ignoring your obligations; rather, it means recognizing the significance of mental rehabilitation.

How can you calm your brain and regain control?

After discussing how stress affects the brain, let's discuss how to manage it constructively.

1. Recognize warning signs early.

The first stage is to learn to identify when your brain is preparing for a stress reaction. You understand your body better than anybody else. So pay attention to the small cues: shallow breathing, clenched fists, and stiff shoulders. When you see yourself becoming physically stiff or emotionally upset, take a break. This is the point at which you can break the cycle before it intensifies.

Begin by doing deep breathing techniques. Inhale deeply through your nose, hold for four counts, and then slowly exhale. This straightforward approach stimulates your body's relaxation response, which calms the amygdala and awakens the prefrontal cortex, the reasoning section of your brain. Deep breathing delivers a signal to your body that says, "Hey, you can relax now."

2. Changing the Narrative: Reframe Your Thoughts

Another effective method for recovering control of your reflexes is to confront the concepts that are racing through your brain. An agitated brain produces a sense of urgency or a "catastrophic" view of the issue. Maybe you believe that if I don't shout right now, my child will not listen to me, or that if I don't do this task, everything will fall apart.

Instead, attempt to reframe these notions. Remind

yourself that this is temporary and prepare to handle it. It is critical to change from an emotional, reactive state to a more reasoned one. This is not always simple, but with practice, it gets easier to halt, rephrase your ideas, and reply calmly.

3. Develop Emotional Resilience via Self-Care.

Taking care of oneself is not a luxury; it is a need. The more you care for your mental and physical health, the more your brain can handle stress. This might include getting more rest, exercising frequently, or finding time for activities that offer you joy and relaxation.

Making self-care a priority is important not only when you're "feeling good" but also during stressful times. More emotional reserves mean more preparedness for difficult situations. Remember that self-care does not have to be a time-consuming activity; it may be as simple as spending a few moments during the day to recharge.

Rewire your brain for calmness.

Your brain's ability to adapt and change is what makes it so amazing. Neuroplasticity refers to your brain's capacity to form new connections and pathways through your experiences. By constantly practicing mindfulness, reframing negative thoughts, and taking efforts to lessen stress, you are physically rebuilding your brain to respond with greater calm and resilience.

As Dr. Daniel Siegel, a top specialist in brain development, once observed, "The mind is what the brain does." It means you can change your brain's reactions, which affect how you parent, handle stress, and support your child.

Understanding your brain's response to stress goes beyond accepting it. It is about giving yourself the skills you need to recover control and respond calmly and clearly, even in the most difficult situations. Understanding how stress affects your body and brain will help you change your behavior and create a peaceful environment for you and your child.

The next time you feel a spike of tension, remember that you are not powerless. Your brain is merely reacting on instinct, but with practice, you can teach yourself to behave in a healthier, more balanced manner. It's a process that will take time, but each tiny step brings you closer to becoming the parent and person you want to be.

Chapter 1 Summary: Let's Understand Why You're Stuck

In this chapter, we went deeply into the root causes of why you may be feeling imprisoned in a cycle of stress and frustration as a parent. Here are the main takeaways.

Yelling is frequently a response to overwhelming stress.

For example, if a child refuses to do their schoolwork after a long day of work and housework, you may become frustrated and snap, unknowingly raising your voice.

Yelling is a reactive behavior that results from mismanaged stress and emotional excess. Understanding how stress influences how you behave might help you start the process of change.

Your brain's stress response might undermine your parenting.

When your child throws a tantrum in the midst of a grocery store, your brain activates the "fight or flight" reaction, making it difficult to remain calm and think properly.

The brain's innate stress reaction might lead to a loss of control in emotionally intense situations. Recognizing this reaction allows you to pause, take a deep breath, and respond calmly.

Your own emotional state strongly influences your triggers.

For example, if you've had a difficult day at work, a minor quarrel with your child may feel like the final straw, making your emotional condition the underlying cause of your outburst.

Recognizing your emotional triggers helps you break the cycle of reactive parenting. When you know what's truly causing your stress, you can start making conscious decisions about how to respond.

Taking breaks and practicing self-care are crucial.

Example: After a difficult morning, taking a few minutes to meditate or just breathe deeply might help you reset your emotional state before reconnecting with your child again.

Exhaustion makes it difficult to maintain patience and emotional clarity with your child. Self-care is not a luxury; it is necessary for effective parenting.

Once you've identified the cause of your shouting and emotional exhaustion, the next step is to take back control of your emotions. In Chapter 2, we'll look at how you may start to regulate your emotions successfully, breaking away from this reactionary loop and creating a calmer, more serene home atmosphere. To modify your responses, self-regulation is crucial, and it starts with understanding how to remain grounded during stressful situations.

In the next chapter, we will go over practical ideas and practices to help you stay in control of your emotions even when stress becomes overwhelming. The route to becoming a more aware and patient parent starts now..

Chapter 2: Take Charge of Your Emotions

"You can't always control what happens around you,
but you can control how you respond."

Frustrated? Here's How to Stay Grounded in the Moment.

It's common to feel overwhelmed when you're trying to balance everything as a parent. There are days when you feel completely exhausted, and even the smallest thing can set you off. Perhaps it's the never-ending laundry, the perpetual clutter in the house, or your child's inability to listen. It seems your patience has been tested, and frustration rises.

And then there's the moment. Your youngster says something that drives you over the brink; your blood pressure rises, and you start yelling. You feel as if you've lost control, and the frustration weighs heavily on you. The toughest thing is the aftermath: guilt. You look at your child and wonder whether you might have done things differently. However, in the intensity of the moment, everything appears to be escalating beyond control.

Does this sound familiar? It's a pattern that many

parents fall into, and it's extremely difficult to stop. However, the good news is that you can break free from this cycle. You may learn how to center yourself in moments of irritation so that you don't lose control.

Staying grounded is more than just a lovely notion; it's a real, concrete skill that may transform how you approach difficult parenting situations. You have the ability to change your emotional state from frustrated to peaceful, from stressed to clear, and from reactive to proactive. This article will discuss its appearance, mechanism, and use in parenting.

<u>The Source of Frustration: Why Are We So Upset?</u>

First, let us figure out why we are irritated in the first place. Parenting is difficult. You are always managing your child's requirements, work responsibilities, domestic tasks, and everything in between. There is a lot to manage. When things do not go as planned, it is simple to become overwhelmed.

However, a mismatch between our expectations and reality often leads to irritation. You would expect your child to be calm and compliant, but they are not. They can be pushing limits or refusing to follow instructions. You feel helpless at that time. You have no control over your child's conduct, and your tolerance is growing thin. When these sensations accumulate, irritation is the normal emotional response.

Another source of dissatisfaction is stress and tiredness. When you're cognitively, emotionally, and physically exhausted, your ability to cope with stress decreases significantly. It's like trying to fill an overflowing cup. Due to your limited stress tolerance, even minor obstacles may seem insurmountable.

The positive news is that once you identify the source of your irritation, you can take actions to successfully manage it.

How to Identify Frustration Early

The first step toward staying grounded is awareness. When you intervene before your frustration escalates, you can control your response. So, how can you know when you're becoming frustrated?

Begin by paying attention to your physical and emotional cues. Bodily symptoms such as increased heart rate, muscular tension, and clenched fists typically accompany frustration. Your mind may begin to speed, and you may feel unable to focus on anything else. If you recognize these shifts early, you can take a break before becoming overwhelmed.

A beneficial practice is to ask yourself the following questions: How am I feeling right now? Am I becoming upset? What does my body tell me? Taking a minute to reflect on your own emotional condition may make a significant impact.

For example, suppose your youngster ignores your request to tidy up. You may become upset at first, but you quickly forget about it. However, as soon as they reject you once more, your frustration intensifies. Your shoulders stiffen, your jaw tightens, and your breathing gets shallow. If you detect these warning signals early on, you will be able to intervene before raising your voice. The idea is to pause before reacting, allowing oneself to respond with intention.

Take a deep breath: The power of pausing.

Taking a deep breath is one of the most effective ways to be present and focused. This basic strategy may sound cliché, but it works. When you take a steady, deep breath, you are physically soothing your nervous system and signaling to your brain to relax. It acts as a reset button for your emotions.

Here's how it works: when you're upset, your body switches to fight-or-flight mode. Your heart rate rises, your muscles stiffen, and your emotions become more intense. However, purposefully slowing your breathing sends a signal to your brain that you are not in danger and are safe. This helps to relax your mind and body.

The next time you feel frustrated, do this: inhale deeply for four counts, hold for four counts, then exhale for four. Try this for a few breaths. As you do, observe how your body begins to relax. Your shoulders may relax, your pulse rate may calm, and you'll probably feel more in control of the situation.

Breathing is a simple yet effective way to restore control, focus yourself, and prevent snapping.

Mindfulness is bringing yourself back to the present moment.

Another important skill for remaining grounded is mindfulness—the practice of paying full attention to the present moment without judgment. Mindfulness involves being present rather than fixating on the past or future.

As a parent, it's simple to become preoccupied with the past or future. You may be rehashing past grievances or worried about potential situations. This removes you from the current moment and raises your tension. However, practicing mindfulness allows you to reconnect with the present moment.

Consider this scenario: you've urged your youngster to put their shoes on three times, and they still refuse. You see your frustration mounting, but instead of responding, try this: pause for a moment, take a breath, and concentrate on what's going on around you. Take note of the sounds in your surroundings, how your body feels, and the room's temperature. This grounding practice can help you focus and escape your thoughts. Once you've completed this, you'll be much better able to reply calmly and effectively.

Reframing Your Thoughts: Altering Your Mental Narrative

Negative thoughts like "I can't handle this anymore" or "This is impossible" typically accompany irritation. These thoughts amplify your irritation and make it more challenging to remain grounded. Instead of letting negative ideas rule you, consider reframing them.

Reframing entails shifting your viewpoint on the circumstance. Instead of thinking, "I'm losing control," try telling yourself, "I'm in charge of how I react." Instead of thinking, "This is too much," think, "This is a challenge, but I can handle it."

Reframing helps you alter your mentality from helplessness to empowerment. It helps you to break away from the emotional spiral and restore control of your responses.

Self-compassion: Be Kind to Yourself.

Finally, remember that remaining grounded does not imply perfection. It's normal to feel frustrated at times. The answer is to engage in self-compassion. When you respond in irritation, instead of beating yourself up, remind yourself that you are human. Accept that you are trying your best and that parenting is difficult.

Self-compassion is the act of treating oneself with the same care and understanding that one would provide to a friend. When you practice self-compassion, you may learn from your mistakes without feeling guilty. This creates opportunities for growth and advancement.

Staying grounded in stressful situations is a skill that requires practice. But with awareness, breathing exercises, mindfulness, and reframing, you may develop the emotional resilience required to remain calm and in control. Remember that while irritation is a natural emotion, you have the ability to choose how you respond. You have the ability to remain grounded and respond patiently, and each time you exercise these skills, you are developing your emotional muscles for future situations.

LEARN HOW YOUR ANGER AFFECTS YOUR CHILD AND BREAK THE CYCLE.

Being a parent can be an emotional journey. On some days, you experience joy, laughter, and a deep connection with your child, while on others, frustration and rage seem to dominate. You may be doing your best to hold things together, but every minor slip-up, every repeated request to "pick up your toys" or "finish your homework," seems like it's slowly shredding your patience. And before you realize it, you're unintentionally raising your voice or screaming. Afterward, you may feel guilty, dejected, and question whether there is a better way to approach things.

This cycle of wrath and remorse affects not just you, but also your child. Despite your belief that your outbursts will "get over it," anger has long-term effects on your relationship with your child. Your rage can influence their behavior, emotional state, and even long-term mental health. If this tendency persists, it could develop into a challenging cycle, inherited from successive generations.

Let's be honest with ourselves: how many times have you yelled in exasperation, only to have your child retreat, act out, or mimic your behavior? It's tempting to believe that a sudden outburst has no long-term ramifications, but the truth is considerably more complicated. By letting anger control your reactions, you may unintentionally teach your child how to handle their emotions. Ending this cycle is crucial for your own well-being and your child's emotional development.

The Hidden Effects of Anger on Your Child

When you become upset, it affects everyone around you, even your child. Children are extremely sensitive to their parents' emotional condition. Children don't require you to yell for them to understand that something is amiss. Even if you believe you are concealing your irritation, people may detect it in your tone, body language, and energy level. You may believe that your anger is justifiable because your child isn't listening or acting out, but it's vital to remember that anger has a direct influence on how your child feels and behaves.

Let me ask you this: How often have you witnessed your child get nervous or distressed as a result of your furious outbursts? Perhaps they shut down, avoid eye contact, or become defensive. Children, particularly younger ones, lack the ability to manage their emotions in the same way that adults do. When you lash out, it can lead to confusion, worry, and insecurity. This is especially true when rage appears unexpected or severe. Your youngster may come to link you with feelings of dread or discomfort, which might eventually form a barrier between you two.

Furthermore, prolonged exposure to anger—whether verbal or physical—can result in long-term emotional and behavioral problems. Children who grow up in angry or mismanaged surroundings are more prone to developing anxiety, depression, or self-regulation disorders. They may struggle to manage their own impulses and may even exhibit aggressive tendencies in their relationships with classmates, instructors, and, eventually, their own children. This is difficult, but we must face it to change our habits and break the cycle.

Why do you become angry?

Before we go into how to interrupt the pattern, we need to understand why anger occurs in the first place. Anger is a normal human emotion—it's your body's response to events that feel unfair, overpowering, or unpleasant. As a parent, you constantly encounter challenges like managing chores, establishing boundaries, managing tantrums, and managing numerous other tasks. When your child refuses to listen or questions your authority, it might feel like they are pushing you to your limits. This causes frustration, which may easily lead to fury.

However, anger is not merely a spontaneous reaction; it often stems from several underlying causes. Stress is a major influence. If you're already feeling overwhelmed by life's obligations, you're more prone to losing control when things don't go as planned. Exhaustion is an additional factor. Parenting is exhausting, especially when you're trying to do it all—work, housework, and meeting your child's demands. When you're exhausted, your tolerance runs away, making it difficult to remain calm.

Finally, unfulfilled needs can cause rage. Resentment is straightforward if you don't feel supported by your spouse or take care of yourself emotionally. Feeling inadequacy or frustration when your child doesn't behave as expected can lead to rage.

How Anger Forms a Cycle

The most difficult aspect of rage is that it does not go away immediately after an outburst. Anger can cause you to become furious, regret your actions, feel guilty, and vow not to do it again. But then the next stressor strikes, and you're back in the same pattern. Over time, this habit shapes your behavior and relationship with your child.

Here's how it normally goes: you become furious, and your child responds in one of two ways. Either they feel agitated, sobbing or withdrawing within themselves, or they act out in reaction, replicating the conduct they have observed from you. In both cases, the cycle deepens. You feel awful about your outburst, but the next time anything provokes you, you respond the same way.

It's straightforward to dismiss this as a hopeless cause, but it's not. Over time, you can acquire and practice awareness, intention, and new coping mechanisms to break the pattern. The first step is to notice when you're becoming upset and take a step back before responding.

Breaking the Cycle: Strategies for Change

Breaking the cycle of rage entails learning how to express your feelings in a healthy way, rather than repressing them. Here's how to get started:

1. Practice self-awareness.

To end the pattern, you must first notice when it is taking place. As we learned before in Chapter 1, frustration and fury can build up gradually. Self-awareness is essential for preventing it before it gets out of control. Begin paying attention to your emotional and physical signs. Notice when your stress levels rise, your muscles stiffen, or your patience runs out. The sooner you catch yourself, the simpler it will be to halt and refocus.

2. Use healthy outlets for your emotions.

Instead of suppressing your anger or allowing it to overflow in a damaging way, discover healthy outlets for your feelings. Exercise, deep breathing, writing, or simply taking a break are all beneficial. If you're feeling overwhelmed, give yourself permission to move away, even if just for five minutes. When you step back, you give yourself time to calm down, reset your perspective, and face the problem with a clearer head.

3. Communicate calmly with your child.

Once you've processed your emotions, gently talk to

your child. This does not imply concealing your emotions, but rather expressing them in a productive rather than negative manner. Instead of shouting, try expressing, "I'm irritated right now because I've asked you to clean up several times and it's not being done. Can we work together to finish this?" This not only demonstrates how to communicate successfully, but it also demonstrates to your child that anger does not have to result in confrontation but rather in collaboration.

4. Model Emotional Regulation.

Your youngster learns from your actions. When you manage your emotions, you are also imparting this knowledge to your child. Emotional regulation is a skill that develops over time, and you may help your child acquire it by modeling how to deal with frustration. When you demonstrate self-control, your kid learns that when they are unhappy, they do not need to respond with anger—they may take a deep breath, talk, and settle the matter quietly.

Breaking the cycle of rage is not about perfection but about progress. Setting a new foundation for your connection involves becoming aware of your triggers, practicing emotional regulation, and giving your kid healthy methods to express emotions. To eliminate all irritation and anger is impossible, but managing them can help you and your child. As you implement these tactics, you will begin to restore your relationship with your kid, resulting in a more tranquil and supportive atmosphere for all concerned.

Remember that your mental health directly affects your child's emotional health. By controlling your emotions, you not only improve your own well-being, but you also provide your kid with the tools they need to manage their own feelings and develop into a confident, emotionally robust adult.

Turn Reactivity into Calm: Your Path to a Peaceful Mindset.

If you're reading this, you've probably had those moments when stress, anger, and frustration overwhelm you and drive you to crack. Perhaps you've yelled at your child over a minor issue like a missed chore or spilled milk, and now you're grappling with a profound sense of guilt, questioning, "Why did I react that way?" Many parents experience this emotion, or cycle of reaction. It's the emotional rollercoaster of life, and it sometimes seems like there's no way out.

What if there was a way to get off the rollercoaster? What if there were a method to transform that knee-jerk emotion into a calm, collected one that preserves your bond with your child and keeps you grounded? You are not alone in this challenge, but response does not have to define your parenting style. You have the ability to change your emotions and reclaim control over your answers. This transition will not occur quickly, but with persistent work and awareness, you can make it a reality.

Let's look at how you might turn your reactions—bursts of rage, impatience, and stress—into calm, calculated replies. This adjustment will not only benefit you, but it will also make your child's surroundings more tranquil and allow both of you to learn healthy conflict resolution strategies.

Why Does Reactivity Happen?

Reactivity is a natural and emotional reaction to stress. It's an impulsive feeling that arises within you without thinking or intention. Our brains naturally exhibit reactivity. We evolved our brains for fast, survival-oriented reflexes. When confronted with stress or perceived threats (such as your child's conduct or a growing list of duties), your brain goes into fight-or-flight mode. This part of your brain automatically reacts without thinking. In those instances, the reaction frequently takes the shape of shouting, snapping, or feeling overwhelmed.

The positive news is that you don't have to follow those responses. You possess the power to step back, maintain composure, and choose a response that aligns with your values and goals as a parent. The first step toward breaking the cycle of reactivity is to understand why it occurs. Without understanding the triggers and patterns, you cannot change them.

The Power of Awareness: Recognizing Your Triggers.

Awareness is the next stage in the path. You cannot modify your reactions unless you understand what causes them. Have you ever found yourself reacting to your child's conduct in ways that didn't seem appropriate for the situation? Perhaps you yelled at something trivial, like your child refusing to follow your cleaning instructions. You might have justified the situation at the time. But you didn't understand there was something deeper going on—possibly a buildup of stress from work, a lack of sleep, or unresolved conflict.

Awareness is critical to stopping the loop. What specific events or actions set you off? Is it when your youngster does not listen immediately? Do they argue with you in public? Perhaps the issue arises when you feel like you've asked the same question a hundred times? Once you've identified your triggers, you'll understand why you behave the way you do. This awareness allows you to make a deliberate decision in the moment rather than allowing your emotions to dictate your answer.

How to Pause and Reset: The Power of Breath and Mindfulness

Sometimes you can't control what happens, but you can react. When you feel your anger or annoyance increasing, the best thing to do is press the stop button. I understand that this seems easier said than done, but it is feasible, and it all starts with a simple tool: breathing.

Take a few deep breaths when you're feeling stressed. This may seem like a minor detail, but it has a significant impact. Breathing activates your parasympathetic nervous system, which calms your body and inhibits the fight-or-flight reaction. Focusing on your breath allows your brain to take a break from the emotional reaction and make room for a more controlled, deliberate response.

Imagine being in front of your child and them disagreeing or not listening. You feel irritated, and your chest tightens. Take a big breath in through the nose and out through the mouth. After a few repetitions, you should notice a decrease in tension. This pause facilitates the shift from an emotional response to a thoughtful response, rooted in calm and intention.

The Power of Perspective: How to Reframe Your Thoughts

After you've halted and recovered emotional control, the next step is to reframe your thinking. Instead of concentrating on your child's misbehavior or how worried you are, take a more balanced approach. Reframing is a method of questioning an original understanding of a situation and adopting a more productive perspective.

For example, suppose your child refuses to complete their schoolwork. In the past, you may have wondered, "Why don't they listen to me?" Why is this so difficult? This kind of thinking might increase irritation. Instead, try phrasing it as "I understand that homework can be difficult." I need to assist them in getting through this in a way that promotes their development and teaches them responsibility.

This difference in viewpoint can have a significant influence on how you handle the circumstance. Avoid the aggravation and focus on the solution and your child's need. Reframing your thinking can also help you build greater empathy for your child's difficulties, making it easier to respond compassionately rather than angrily.

Self-Talk: The Power of Kindness.

Positive self-talk is the next strong strategy you may use to achieve tranquility. You've probably heard this term before, but it's crucial for learning to shift from a reactive state to a calm one. The way you talk to yourself during times of stress has a significant influence on how you respond to your child.

What do you tell yourself when you feel your frustration rising? Are you thinking, "I can't manage this," or "It's impossible?" Or are you telling yourself, "I got this, and I can handle it calmly."

Your inner conversation has a major impact on how you see the circumstance. Negative self-talk can increase emotions of powerlessness and irritation, whereas positive self-talk promotes resilience and serenity. One strong sentence to remember in stressful situations is, "I am in control of my response." Reminding yourself of this helps you stay grounded when things don't go as planned.

Modeling Calm for Your Child.

As you work on developing a tranquil mentality, keep in mind that your child is observing you. Demonstrate to them how you manage stress. If you can regulate your emotions in a calm and measured manner, your child will soon learn the same abilities.

Consider the influence on your child's emotional development when they watch you take a deep breath, pause, and reply with patience. Children learn from you to understand and manage emotions, not fear or suppress them. This is a crucial lesson for any youngster, since it helps them develop emotional intelligence, which will benefit them throughout their lives.

Turning reactivity into serenity is a lifetime exercise, not a quick remedy. The methods we've discussed—self-awareness, breathing, reframing, positive self-talk, and modeling calm—are all critical stages in changing your perspective and emotional responses. You are learning to transition from reaction to conscious response, and each time you practice these abilities, you strengthen your foundation for emotional control.

Remember, change does not occur overnight. It requires time, patience, and persistent work. However, when you begin to apply these tactics in your daily life, you will notice a change. You'll respond less impulsively, be more present in the moment, and, most importantly, develop a deeper, more connected relationship with your child.

We'll discuss how parents and children need emotional regulation in the next section. Continue to use these skills, and remember that you have the ability to mold your reaction and, ultimately, your family's emotional environment.

<u>Summary of Chapter 2: Take Charge of Your Emotions.</u>

Understand Your Emotions: Recognizing and

understanding your emotions is the first step toward gaining control.

For example, before reacting to your child's unwillingness to tidy their room, you admit your displeasure and identify the underlying cause—being overwhelmed by a busy day. This knowledge allows you to remain calm rather than lash out.

Breaking the Cycle of Reactivity: Reacting without thinking simply increases the strain.

For example, when your child fights with you, instead of instantly raising your voice, you take a deep breath, ground yourself, and choose to approach the matter gently, demonstrating emotional control.

Converting Reactivity into Calm: With practice, you may transform your reactive behavior into a deliberate, calm reaction.

For example, at a difficult time, you pause, focus on your breath, and choose to speak to your child patiently, de-escalating the situation and teaching your child how to deal with frustration constructively.

Reframe negative thoughts: Changing your perception affects your emotional response.

When your child refuses to listen, instead of thinking, "I can't take this anymore," you reframe the situation as, "This is a chance to teach patience and understanding." This perspective helps you stay calm and present.

Positive self-talk: How you communicate with yourself impacts how you manage your emotions.

For example, in the middle of turmoil, you tell yourself, "I am capable of staying calm," and this affirmation keeps you grounded, averting an emotional outburst.

Modeling Calm for Your Child: Your emotional responses educate your youngster on how to regulate their own emotions.

When confronted with a stressful scenario, instead of shouting, you calmly explain the problem to your child, demonstrating that emotional control is possible even in difficult situations.

Self-compassion and patience: Being gentle with yourself when you make errors allows you to grow.

For example, instead of beating yourself up after an emotional reaction, you own your error and focus on learning from it in order to do better the next time.

Be aware that how you regulate your emotions affects your relationship with your child as you study emotional regulation and parenting. As you begin to develop a tranquil mentality, it's important to shift your attention from controlling emotions to developing deeper relationships with your family.

In the following chapter, we'll look at how to utilize emotional control as a basis for creating trust, connection, and stronger ties within your family.

Chapter 3: Build Stronger Connections with Your Family

"The quality of your relationships determines the quality of your life." — Robbins, Tony.

STOP THE CONFLICT: LEARN EFFECTIVE PARENTING STRATEGIES.

Consider this scenario: Your youngster is pressing every button. They refuse to perform their chores, argue with their siblings, and nothing you say seems to help. You feel like you're going to snap. This is more than simply a terrible day; it seems like a never-ending loop. The aggravation grows, the fight increases, and you think, "Why is this happening again?"

This sort of constant confrontation is draining for both you and your child. You may feel ensnared in an unbreakable cycle. The positive news is that you don't have to stay stuck. You can break the pattern, reduce stress, and create an environment where both you and your child feel heard, respected, and understood.

Understanding Conflict: What Really Happens?

Before discussing methods, we must understand the background. Unmet needs and inadequate communication are frequently the sources of conflict. As parents, we sometimes think that our children should "know better" or appreciate the value of rules and routines. Children are still learning how to manage their emotions, communicate their wants, and deal with frustration. Conflicts are more likely to occur when people lack the ability to communicate properly.

The same goes for us as parents. Anxiety, overwork, or exhaustion depletes our emotional reserves. This makes it more difficult to stay calm and patient when disagreement arises. We're more inclined to respond impulsively, exacerbating the problem.

Parenting Strategies: Ending the Conflict

Now that we understand why disagreements arise, let us look at some practical techniques for resolving them and building better, healthier connections with your children.

1. Active Listening: Help Your Child Feel Heard

The first step in resolving disagreement is to ensure your youngster feels heard. Active listening is one of the most effective parenting strategies. Beyond hearing what they say, you must understand their emotions and needs. Children who sense their attention are less inclined to escalate the issue.

When participating in active listening, concentrate on the following areas:

- Empathy: Recognize your child's feelings. If they are upset, think about their emotions. Consider saying something like, "I can see that you're really upset about not being able to play with your toys right now."
- Nonjudgmental attitude: Refrain from rushing to conclusions or forming assumptions. Listen without judging.
- Presence: Put down your phone, switch off the television, and give your child your whole attention.
- The more you practice active listening, the better you'll be at responding to your child's needs without escalating conflict. It allows your youngster to feel understood and validated.

2. Set clear and consistent boundaries.

Setting clear and consistent boundaries is another effective method for resolving conflict. When there are clear rules in place, children feel safe and flourish. Clear expectations eliminate uncertainty and help prevent power clashes.

Consistency is essential when creating limits. If you say no one day and allow it the next, your child may question the rules. For instance, if you limit screen usage to 30 minutes per day, make sure to consistently adhere to this restriction. If you let your child watch TV longer one day because you're weary, they'll start to push the boundaries, which might lead to more problems.

Setting boundaries, however, should not imply rigidity or inflexibility. Be open to conversation, and attempt to provide options wherever feasible. Instead of stating, "You need to clean your room now," you may add, "You can clean it now or after dinner." Which do you prefer?" This provides your youngster a sense of control while reducing resistance.

3. Positive Reinforcement: Catch them being good.

Positive reinforcement is a highly effective method for minimizing conflict. It focuses on rewarding desired actions rather than penalizing undesirable behaviors. When you notice your child doing something great, be sure to acknowledge it. This makes children feel appreciated and respected, motivating them to continue their excellent habits.

For instance, express your gratitude by saying, "I really appreciate how you helped set the table today," if your child does so without asking. That was wonderful assistance!" Positive reinforcement improves children's self-esteem and deepens the parent-child relationship.

Psychologist B.F. Skinner's research study showed that positive reinforcement significantly outperforms punishment in encouraging desirable actions. The objective is to reinforce positive conduct rather than simply pointing out negative behavior.

4. Time for everyone: Take breaks to reset.

It's critical to recognize that sometimes the best approach to resolve a dispute is to take a break. When emotions are strong, taking a break from the situation might help you and your child reset. This is not about punishing your child or ignoring the issue. It's about giving both of you room to relax and get perspective.

You may execute this method by instituting "time-outs" for all parties involved, not just the youngster. Tell and encourage your child to take a break when they become frustrated. This may include each of you spending five minutes sitting quietly, breathing, or engaging in a relaxing activity such as reading or painting.

On your second encounter, you'll be calmer and ready to resolve the conflict.

5. Collaborative problem-solving: Work together to find solutions.

Instead of arguing about who is right or wrong, adopt a collaborative problem-solving method. Instead of pushing your will on your child, encourage him or her to participate in the solution. This helps kids develop critical thinking abilities and prepares them to deal with future disagreements.

If your child refuses to finish schoolwork, ask, "What do you think we can do to make schoolwork simpler for you?" This encourages communication and empowers your youngster to identify answers.

Collaborative problem-solving fosters trust and supports the notion that you're a team working toward a common objective.

6. Manage Your Emotions: Be the Role Model.

Children learn by example; therefore, it's critical that you regulate your own emotions well. If you react to problems with anger, impatience, or harsh words, your child is likely to follow suit. Alternatively, your child will learn serenity and emotional management from you.

When you are frustrated, take a minute to pause and breathe. You may model this process for your kid by stating, "I'm feeling upset right now, so I'm going to take a deep breath and calm down before we talk." Your child gains insight into the normality of emotions and the ability to regulate them through healthy methods.

Stopping conflict needs more than one-time remedies. It is about developing a mentality and tactics to establish a foundation of respect, understanding, and trust in your connection with your child. By continuously employing active listening, setting clear limits, implementing positive reinforcement, and encouraging cooperation, you may build a tranquil environment that lowers conflict and enhances your relationship.

Parenting isn't about avoiding all conflicts; it's about knowing how to handle them properly. The more you use these tactics, the simpler it will be to face obstacles in a calm and productive manner. Remember that it's alright to make errors. What is important is your desire to learn, grow, and have a wonderful relationship with your child.

Do you want more trust and love in your home? Let's build it.

Have you ever had a nagging sense of disconnect between yourself and your child? Perhaps they appear reclusive, unwilling to confide in you, or more prone to challenge your authority. You want to establish a solid, loving connection, but it seems like something is getting in the way. The positive news is that you can completely shift the dynamic. You can build a household full of trust and love, but it will require purposeful work, patience, and a little forethought.

Recent family psychology studies show that children's experiences with empathy, consistency, and emotional safety significantly influence their confidence in their parents. Dr. John Gottman, one of the most prominent specialists in family dynamics, discovered that children who feel understood and supported by their parents are more likely to acquire high levels of self-esteem and emotional intelligence. Is your family lacking trust and love? You're not alone, but you can change it.

<u>Trust plays a crucial role in parent-child relationships.</u>

Trust is the cornerstone of all healthy relationships, including the parent-child link. Without trust, your relationship with your child becomes unstable. Trust helps your kid to feel comfortable expressing themselves, sharing their opinions, and communicating openly. Without it, people may withdraw emotionally and keep things pent up within. This can cause greater tension, conflict, and isolation.

However, how can you repair damaged trust or fortify existing trust? The answer is a consistent, purposeful strategy, which begins with you.

<u>How to Build Trust: Show Your Child That You Are Reliable.</u>

One of the most important components of establishing trust with your child is proving that you are a dependable and continuous presence in their life. Children must trust you physically and emotionally to be there when you say you will. If you consistently breach promises or respond unpredictably to their conduct, they may lose faith in you.

Begin with little promises—such as "We'll spend time together after dinner" or "I'll be here when you get home from school." Keep such commitments regularly. Trust does not develop immediately, but with time and frequent pleasant interactions, your youngster will feel more safe in your company.

Assume your youngster has been requesting you to play a board game with them all week. You keep telling them you're too busy, yet deep down you know they really need your attention. Finally, you make time to sit down with them, arriving as promised. Although small, this act shows your child that they can trust you. It helps them gain the trust they need to feel safe and cherished.

How can you develop empathy and understanding in your parenting?

One of the best ways to improve your relationship with your child is empathy. When you show empathy, you tell your child that their feelings matter. Empathy, more than just listening to your child, involves acknowledging their emotions.

According to child development research, children who get empathy from their parents are more likely to form solid bonds and have a higher sense of self-worth. They also learn to manage their emotions in a better way.

Mirroring your child's feelings is an effortless technique to develop empathy. If your child is sad because they did not get what they wanted, instead of dismissing it or encouraging them to "get over it," say something like, "I see you're quite disappointed right now. I'd feel the same if I didn't get what I wanted." This simple phrase can have a profound impact on your child, as it communicates your awareness and understanding of them.

Creating Emotional Safety: The Importance of Consistency

Consistency is essential for developing trust and

emotional safety. Children feel comfortable when they know what to expect from their surroundings and people. If your child is unsure how you will behave in a specific scenario, it might cause worry and mistrust.

One of the most effective ways to achieve consistency is to establish family rituals and norms that everyone adheres to. Having a fixed bedtime schedule, frequent family dinners, or consistent screen time regulations can all help your youngster feel more stable. When children understand what to anticipate, they feel more safe and are more likely to participate enthusiastically.

This does not require you to establish a rigid, unyielding family structure. Flexibility is also vital. But when you set clear standards and stick to them, your child will realize that the rules apply to everyone, including you. This constancy builds trust.

Make Time for Connection: Prioritize Quality over Quantity.

Building trust and love in your household does not require spending every waking second with your children. It's about the quality of your time together. In reality, research suggests that youngsters favor genuine connections above hours of idle time spent together. The moments when you are totally present and engaged will have the most influence.

Make it a priority to schedule one-on-one time with your youngster. This might be as simple as having a peaceful conversation before bed, creating a meal together, or doing something they like. What matters most is that you are totally engaged and without distractions. Put down the phone, switch off the television, and show your child that they are your priority.

For example, if your child enjoys sketching, spend time with them drawing together. Ask them questions about their artwork and pay close attention to what they say. You show concern for their interests and build an emotional bond.

Positive Reinforcement: Encourage trust with positive feedback.

Positive reinforcement is an excellent method for encouraging behaviors that foster trust. Take the time to acknowledge and reward your child's responsible or emotionally mature behavior. As you focus on the positive, your child will feel loved and valued.

For example, if your child expresses their feelings in a healthy way rather than acting out, congratulate them for doing so. You may remark, "I'm so proud of you for telling me how you feel instead of yelling." That helps me understand you better.

The more positive feedback you give your child for trust-building activities, the more likely they are to repeat them. Positive reinforcement enhances your child's sense of security by reassuring them of your attention and appreciation.

Modeling Trust and Respect: Lead by Example.

As a parent, you are your child's first role model. The way you interact with others, handle disagreement, and express your emotions will influence how your kid learns to navigate relationships. If you want your child to trust you, you must demonstrate trustworthiness yourself.

When you make errors (and you will), be open about them. Apologize when appropriate, and teach your child that making errors is a normal part of being human. Modeling vulnerability may increase trust because your child views you as a genuine person, not simply an authoritative figure.

You shouldn't ignore your anger and yell at your child. After you've cooled down, go to them and apologize for shouting before. I became irritated, and I should not have raised my voice. I want us to discuss quietly when we disagree." This teaches your youngster that it's alright to make mistakes and how to rebuild connections when trust is broken.

Building trust and love in your household takes effort, but the results are long-lasting. You may foster love and trust in your household by exercising empathy, being consistent, creating time for connection, and praising trust-building actions. The foundation you lay today will result in greater ties with your child tomorrow.

HOW TO STAY CALM AND IN CONTROL WHEN IT MATTERS MOST

Imagine this: Your child has just spilled a full cup of juice on the kitchen floor, and your phone rings with a critical business call. Your mind raced, irritation mounted, and your body tensed up. Your patience quickly diminishes. In moments like this, it's simple to lose control of your emotions, but what if you could learn to remain calm even when everything seems to be coming apart? The American Psychological Association's recent study found that parents who maintain composure under pressure significantly increase their children's likelihood of developing emotional resilience. But how can you improve this critical skill? Let's go exploring.

Why Keeping Calm Matters: A Parent's Emotional Influence

Emotions are infectious. As a parent, your emotional responses have a direct influence on the climate in your house. The anger, irritation, or worry you show affects you and your child. Kids are extremely sensitive to their parents' moods, and they frequently imitate your behaviors, especially in high-stress circumstances. So, if you want your child to acquire emotional control and learn how to deal with adversity, it begins with you.

Consider this: When you lose control, your child may not only feel uneasy, but they will also miss out on witnessing an effective model of emotional regulation. In contrast, remaining cool and composed in difficult situations demonstrates emotional strength and perseverance. You show kids how to approach life's issues carefully rather than impulsively.

But, let's face it: maintaining calm is easier said than done, especially when you're feeling stressed. It takes practice, strategy, and a desire to take charge of your mental condition.

<u>Understanding Your Triggers: What Sets You Off?</u>

Before you can develop the ability to remain calm, you must first understand what causes your emotional reactions. Is the house a mess? A disobedient child? Do the regular responsibilities of work and home life add up? Every parent has triggers that push them beyond their limits. Recognizing these triggers before they intensify is essential for maintaining control.

Consider the scenarios that are most likely to cause annoyance or fury. Write them down if it helps. It's possible that your youngster refuses to do their schoolwork or is talking back while you're already anxious. Identifying your triggers allows you to build ways of dealing with them calmly.

You may get annoyed if your child interrupts an important call. The next time it happens, pause, take a deep breath, and remind yourself that your response is more important than the interruption. Setting limits, such as allowing your child "quiet time" when you need to focus, can help minimize frustrated outbursts.

<u>The Power of Pause: Consider Stepping Back Before Reacting</u>

In times of stress, the most crucial tool you have is the pause button. When you feel your anger or annoyance mounting, avoid the temptation to respond impulsively. Instead, take a few seconds to breathe and collect your thoughts. A brief pause can distinguish between a hasty decision and a thoughtful one.

Dr. Andrew Weil, a top specialist in mind-body health, invented the "4-7-8" breathing technique, which is well-known. To practice, inhale for four seconds, hold for seven seconds, then exhale for eight seconds. This simple breathing method triggers your parasympathetic nervous system, which helps relax your body and lessen stress.

Try pausing the next time you feel overwhelmed, whether it's due to your child's behavior or an unpleasant situation at home. Concentrate on your breath. Remind yourself that you can manage your emotional response. You do not need to react right away. In fact, stopping before responding is one of the most effective ways to stay calm.

Reframe Your Perspective: See the Situation from a Different Angle.

Another excellent way to keep calm is to reframe the issue. Often, we respond emotionally because we perceive the event as a personal assault or something beyond our control. You may find the situation less frustrating if you change your perspective.

Consider a scenario where your child persistently requests something you've previously declined. It's simple to become irritated, especially if you're already feeling exhausted. However, rather than perceiving it as an act of disobedience, consider your child's point of view. They may want your attention or not understand why you said "no."

When you reframe the scenario in this manner, you can assist in lowering your emotional charge. You can tell yourself, "My child is only testing the boundaries right now. It's part of their growth, and I'm here to support them." This simple adjustment in perspective can help you remain calm and patient.

Use "I" statements to communicate calmly and effectively.

When dealing with disagreement, particularly with children, it is critical to communicate in a way that does not exacerbate the problem. Using "I" remarks rather than "you" statements can help you maintain control of your emotions and avoid putting the other person on the defensive.

Instead of stating, "You never listen to me," try saying, "I feel frustrated when I have to repeat myself." This technique focuses on your feelings rather than condemning the other person, and it fosters a more productive discourse.

"I" statements are an effective technique for not just resolving conflicts but also teaching your child how to communicate their emotions in a calm, non-confrontational manner. When people see you exhibit this conduct, they are more inclined to follow suit.

<u>Recognize when to take a break: Self-care is key.</u>

There will be moments when you sense yourself on the verge of breaking. In these circumstances, it is critical to know when you require a break. Stepping away from an uncomfortable situation is not a show of weakness; rather, it is an act of self-care and awareness.

If you feel you are about to lose control, tell your youngster calmly that you need a few seconds to gather your thoughts. You can say something like, "I'm very upset right now, and I need to take a deep breath." "Let's talk in five minutes." This helps you to relax and avoid saying or doing anything you'll regret later.

Pauses are not just for times of conflict. If you're feeling overwhelmed by your parenting obligations, it's beneficial to take a break and recharge. Self-care, whether it's a brief stroll, a cup of tea, or simply five minutes of quiet time, is critical for managing your emotions.

<u>To create a calm environment, reduce external stressors.</u>

Finally, having a tranquil setting might help you maintain control. A chaotic, congested workplace can cause tension and dissatisfaction. Take measures to simplify and tidy your house to eliminate unneeded distractions and pressures.

For example, set aside places for homework, food, and rest. Encourage your youngster to help keep common places neat. A peaceful and ordered workplace can help relieve tension and establish a sense of order, making it easier to retain emotional control when stress levels rise.

Staying calm and in control when it counts most is a continuous exercise. Instead of being perfect, identify and improve your emotional responses. Understanding your triggers, communicating effectively, and prioritizing self-care can allow you to keep control in high-pressure circumstances while also modeling emotional resilience for your child.

As you continue to create these tactics, keep in mind that you are not only avoiding confrontation; you are also laying the groundwork for a lifetime of trust, respect, and emotional intelligence. Your youngster learns from you every day. The more you lead with calm and patience, the more people will adopt those traits in their own lives.

Key Points from Chapter 3: Strengthening Connections with Your Family

- Stop the conflict: learn parenting strategies that work.

For example, if your child refuses to perform their tasks,

utilizing calm disciplinary tactics such as positive reinforcement rather than punishment might encourage collaboration. Instead of controlling, teach to build trust and respect with your child.

Do you want more trust and love in your home? Let's build it.

If your child doesn't trust you, be consistent in words and actions. Keep your promises. Trust is based on dependability and honesty, which builds your family ties over time.

The primary quote is: "Trust is the foundation of all strong relationships—if you build it, love will grow naturally."

* How to stay calm and in control when it matters most

Instead of shouting when your child makes a mistake, employ the "pause and breathe" strategy to restore your calm. This break lets you think before you act and teaches your child to express dissatisfaction calmly.

As we move into Chapter 4, it's time to prioritize self-care. A strong, peaceful family begins with a healthy, balanced parent. Let's look at how self-care and emotional growth may help you be the greatest version of yourself and, by implication, a better parent.

Chapter 4: Take Care of Yourself and Grow Together

"You're stronger than you think."

Feeling drained? Here's How to Reclaim Your Energy.

Parenting is a difficult job, and let's be honest: there doesn't always seem to be enough energy. You wake up early, work hard, take care of your family, and go to bed to do it again. This cycle eventually takes its toll. If you're experiencing exhaustion, you're not alone.

Consider the experience of actor and parent, Dwayne "The Rock" Johnson. Despite his physically demanding job, Johnson has frequently discussed how he manages his hectic work schedule with family life. In interviews, he has emphasized the importance of prioritizing his mental and physical health to prevent burnout. Without care, your body will run out of energy," he says. This is an important lesson for parents: you can't keep giving without replenishing your own tank.

So, what do you do when you feel exhausted? The solution is not as simple as taking a nap (although sleep is necessary). Reclaiming your energy entails many steps, including taking a step back, identifying the reasons for your weariness, and making deliberate, positive choices to restore what you've lost.

<u>Determine the sources of your energy drains.</u>

Understanding where your energy is going is crucial before we start working on solutions. Are you physically exhausted from chasing after your children, dealing with never-ending tasks, or staying up too late trying to do everything? Or are you emotionally exhausted from the continual need to manage family relationships, deal with professional stress, and keep a positive attitude? Often, the problem is a mix of variables.

Identify the source of your energy depletion. Is it your children's incessant needs, your long to-do list, or the emotional strain of trying to keep everything together? You can't cure something you can't recognize. Begin by jotting down particular events or tasks that make you feel fatigued. From there, you may work on setting limits and developing self-care routines that address those specific energy drains.

<u>Self-care is not selfish; it's essential.</u>

When you're exhausted, it's tempting to believe that taking time for yourself is selfish. But the fact is that self-care is more than a luxury; it is a need. You cannot pour from an empty cup, as the phrase goes. To care for your family and be the greatest parent you can be, you must first care for yourself.

Physical self-care might help you start recovering your vitality. For example, many parents, particularly those with small children, are willing to forego sleep in order to accomplish their goals. However, studies reveal that not only does a lack of sleep leave you physically weary, but it also influences your emotional management and cognitive performance. Prioritize getting enough sleep every night. Try creating a peaceful nighttime routine that includes limiting screen time, relaxing with a book, and making sure your surroundings are conducive to deep, restful sleep.

Exercise can replenish your energy.

Physical activity is another technique to replenish your energy reserves. Although paradoxical, exercising while exhausted is one of the best ways to boost energy. Regular physical exercise causes your body to create endorphins, which are natural mood enhancers. It also lowers stress, improves sleep quality, and boosts energy levels.

You don't have to run a marathon or spend an hour at the gym every day to achieve this. Begin small—go for a 20-minute stroll after dinner, do some mild stretching in the morning, or try a quick yoga session. Consistency is essential. As you exercise, your body grants you energy for daily tasks.

Practice mindfulness and stress-reduction techniques.

In addition to physical self-care, mental and emotional well-being play a crucial role in regaining your vitality.

Emotional depletion can be more taxing than physical fatigue. Mindfulness activities such as deep breathing, meditation, and basic relaxation exercises can help you clear your thoughts and replenish your emotional reserves.

One of the most basic strategies is deep breathing. Taking five minutes every day to focus on your breath may make a huge difference. Try this: sit quietly, close your eyes, and breathe deeply through your nose for four counts. Hold your breath for four counts before gently exhaling. Repeat this practice for five minutes, and you'll feel more centered and less emotionally exhausted.

Delegate and ask for assistance.

Another critical component is learning to delegate and seek assistance. Many parents, particularly those who are juggling several responsibilities, attempt to do everything alone. This contributes to burnout. But remember, you don't have to do everything. Asking for help demonstrates strength, not weakness. If you need help, don't hesitate to contact your spouse, a friend, or a relative.

For instance, if you're feeling overwhelmed by housework, consider sharing tasks with your partner. If your children are old enough, engage them in age-appropriate activities. Ask for assistance with errands, or consider hiring someone to help with cleaning or childcare for a few hours each week. Even tiny amounts of assistance may alleviate a lot of burden.

Reframe your mindset and focus on the positive.

Often, the way we think about our circumstances

exacerbates feelings of weariness. If you keep telling yourself, "I'm too tired," or "I can't handle this anymore," you'll create a self-fulfilling prophecy. Changing your mentality might help you regain your energy. Instead of dwelling on the negativity, attempt to reframe your ideas.

For example, instead of thinking, "I'm exhausted; I can't do this," try stating, "I'm tired, but I can take small breaks throughout the day to recharge." This simple change helps stop the loop of negativity and empowers you to act. Reframing your perspective might help you gain control of the situation rather than allowing it to overwhelm you.

Reconnect With Your Purpose.

It's easy to forget why you're doing this when you're exhausted. Reconnecting with your mission might give you motivation to keep going. Consider why you become a parent and the ideals you wish to teach in your children. Reaffirm your aspirations as parents and individuals. Recognizing your mission can give you the energy to endure even the hardest days.

Start small and build consistency.

Reclaiming your energy takes time, just like any other lifestyle adjustment. Begin small and focus on making gradual improvements that are effective for you. Commit to one new behavior, such as going to bed early, getting some exercise, or practicing mindfulness, and stay with it for a few weeks. As your consistency increases, you'll feel more enthusiastic, focused, and balanced.

Remember: this is a marathon, not a sprint. Be patient

with yourself as you embark on this trip. Every modest effort toward self-care and energy restoration adds up.

Many parents experience fatigue at times, but it doesn't have to persist indefinitely. Prioritizing self-care, learning to delegate, practicing mindfulness, and retraining your perspective can help you recapture the energy you need to be the greatest version of yourself for your family. It's time to refill your cup and pour into others.

STRUGGLING TO STOP YELLING? LET'S BREAK THAT HABIT NOW!

We have all been there. The stress of everyday life builds up, irritation increases, and before you realize it, the words fly out—louder than you planned, harsher than you want. At that moment, yelling seems to be your sole means of communicating with your child. But deep down, you know it's not helping. It does not promote connection or understanding. Instead, it leaves you both feeling exhausted and distant. And, most crucially, you may observe how it affects your child—fear, bewilderment, grief, or even fury. The pattern is taxing, and breaking it may be intimidating.

Consider the experience of acclaimed actor Will Smith. Known for his blockbuster performances and his charismatic demeanor, Smith has also openly shared his feelings of wrath and frustration, particularly in his family life. In his memoir, he discusses times when he raised his voice—moments he bitterly regretted because, rather than teaching his children anything vital, he created emotional distance. "The most important thing is teaching your children the lessons that you didn't learn," he says. "And that means learning how to communicate without screaming." Smith's insight is a poignant reminder that yelling, while often intuitive, does not result in the beneficial change we need in our families.

The positive news is that you can break the deeply ingrained habit of yelling that many parents have. If you're trying to quit shouting, you're not alone—and there is help. The trick is to understand why you shout in the first place, to learn better alternatives, and, most importantly, to allow yourself to change and grow. Let us break this habit together.

<u>Why do we yell? Understanding the Root Causes</u>

Before you can stop shouting, you must understand why. Feelings of overload, misunderstanding, or powerlessness frequently motivate yelling. It's a reaction to stress and irritation that, in the heat of the moment, seems like the only way to recover control. In reality, it frequently indicates that we aren't adequately controlling our own emotions.

It's tempting to believe that screaming is a quick fix for catching your child's attention, but in reality, it frequently causes more issues than it helps. Research suggests that persistent screaming or severe discipline can lead to anxiety, low self-esteem, and poor emotional control in children. So, while screaming may result in temporary silence or obedience, it does not promote respect, trust, or beneficial communication.

As a parent, it's critical to go deeper into why you shout. Do you feel overwhelmed by your child's behavior? Are you worried about work or other responsibilities? Do you think your youngster isn't listening to or respecting your authority? Identifying the source of your dissatisfaction is the first step toward stopping the loop.

<u>The Immediate Effects of Yelling on Your Child and You</u>

Yelling can have long-term implications for both you and your child. When you shout, you may believe that you are communicating well, but youngsters frequently tune out strong tones. They may become defensive or emotionally closed off, making it difficult for them to grasp the lesson you are attempting to impart. Yelling is more than simply a source of tension; it may damage trust and emotional safety in your connection with your child.

Think about how you feel after screaming. Sure, there's a sense of relief after the outburst. Maybe you've resolved your dissatisfaction, but are you happy with your handling? More often than not, we feel guilty, regretful, or dissatisfied in ourselves. In those situations, it's easy to forget we can break the cycle before it starts. Understanding the emotional toll that screaming has on both you and your child will encourage you to make long-term improvements.

<u>Rethink Your Approach: Why Yelling Doesn't Work.</u>

The first step toward breaking the habit of yelling is to recognize that it does not work in the long run. While it may briefly focus your child's attention, it does not teach them how to manage their emotions or communicate properly. Yelling is a reactionary activity, not a deliberate one. If you want to educate your child about self-control, empathy, and respect, you must model such characteristics yourself.

One of the most effective ways to handle the issue of shouting is to redefine your perspective on discipline. Instead of considering shouting as a tool for regulating behavior, consider it a signal that you need to halt and manage your own emotions first. It's critical to step back before reacting so you can reply in a way that reflects the values you want to impart in your child.

<u>Create a pause between frustration and reaction.</u>

A simple yet effective method for eliminating the habit of screaming is to create a pause between your aggravation and your reply. This stop allows you to check in with yourself: Are you hungry, fatigued, or stressed? Are you reacting to anything your child did, or is your displeasure stemming from something else in life? Taking a few seconds to consider before responding will help you make more intelligent and successful decisions.

You may also utilize this time to take deep breaths and reset your emotions. For example, if you notice yourself becoming upset, pause for five seconds, take a deep breath, and gently exhale. This mindfulness exercise can help quiet your nervous system and generate the emotional space you need to respond with patience and understanding.

<u>Practice calm and clear communication.</u>

After you've given yourself a minute to reflect, the next stage is to communicate calmly and clearly. It is critical to remember that your tone and body language have a significant influence on how your child interprets your message. Speaking in a calm, steady tone helps you stay in control of the issue without escalating it further.

Instead of yelling, you could say something like, "I need you to stop that behavior right now because it's not safe," or "I'm upset that you didn't listen to me, and I need you to pay attention." Clear communication facilitates your child's understanding of expectations without infusing the situation with emotional drama. It also demonstrates courteous communication, which your youngster may emulate in their own encounters.

<u>Embrace empathy and connection.</u>

Another step to quitting the screaming habit is to embrace empathy. When your child acts out, it's natural to become frustrated or angry. Kids often act out because they're struggling with their emotions or needs. Instead of viewing the behavior as an intended challenge to your authority, consider it a chance to connect with your child and learn how they're feeling.

For example, if your child is having a tantrum because they are exhausted or hungry, you may reply by stating, "I see you're sad right now. Let's take a pause and find out what you need." Demonstrating empathy helps settle the situation and creates an environment in which your child feels heard and understood rather than terrified or dominated.

Consistency and patience are key.

Breaking the habit of screaming takes time, so be patient with yourself. Consistency is essential—every time you pause before reacting or choose calm conversation over screaming, you reinforce new, better patterns of behavior. It won't happen quickly, but with practice, you'll discover that you can better regulate your emotions and create a more pleasant home atmosphere.

Remember, you don't have to be flawless. You will make mistakes from time to time, and that is acceptable. What is important is that you continue working toward your objective. Be kind to yourself during the process, and realize that each step forward is a win.

Breaking the habit of screaming requires more than just emotional control; it also requires setting a positive example. You may teach your child important life skills by learning to manage your own frustration, talk calmly, and respond with empathy. You are demonstrating to children that there is always a better way to manage disagreement and frustration—one that does not entail shouting or fear.

You're Stronger Than You Think: Find Your Inner Power

Consider the instances when you confronted a challenge that felt too large, too overpowering, or just unattainable. Perhaps it was a challenging talk with your child, a rough day at work, or a moment when you felt absolutely exhausted and unsure if you could continue. In those moments, doubt sets in, and a voice within your brain whispers, "I can't do this anymore." What if I told you that you are considerably stronger than you realize? Could it be that you already possess the strength to overcome every challenge, just waiting to discover and unlock it?

Take actor and producer Dwayne "The Rock" Johnson, for example. Johnson, known for his impressive body and strong on-screen attitude, has frequently opened up about his childhood challenges, notably moments of intense sadness and uncertainty. In interviews, Johnson has candidly shared his experience of reaching a low point in his life and feeling as though he had no more to offer. But Johnson did not remain there. He pushed deep and discovered an inner power that catapulted him to success in ways he could not have anticipated. As he puts it, "The struggle and the journey are where your power lies." You can't always control what happens, but you can affect your response."

Like Johnson, you have an amazing store of strength within you. The key to harnessing it is to recognize it, believe in your capacity to deal with life's obstacles, and learn how to nurture it so that it becomes a driving force in your daily life. Today, we will discuss how to discover and utilize your inner power, particularly during times when you feel depleted.

<u>The inner strength you already possess</u>

It's straightforward to believe that those who seem to have everything under control, exude confidence, or handle challenging situations with apparent ease are the ones who possess strength. However, inner strength is not a unique quality that certain individuals are born with. You already have it within you. You've felt it before, even if you didn't realize it at the time. Consider the last time you dealt with a challenging situation—perhaps you remained cool during a stressful family moment or solved a seemingly insurmountable challenge. This was your inner strength at work.

Most individuals don't know that inner strength

functions similarly to a muscle. It becomes stronger as you use it. And the greatest part? You don't have to wait till a crisis to use it. With experience, you may use that strength in everyday situations, especially when you need it the most.

Embracing the power of resilience.

Resilience is a fundamental component of inner strength that we can all acquire. Resilience is defined as the ability to recover from setbacks, learn from failure, and keep moving forward in the face of challenges. As a parent, you are already demonstrating resilience each day. Every time you rise from a challenging day or navigate a challenging situation with your children, you are demonstrating resilience.

Malala Yousafzai, the youngest Nobel Prize recipient, exemplifies resilience. Malala did not give up after surviving the Taliban's murder attempt; instead, she grew even more motivated to fight for girls' education throughout the world. Her tale demonstrates that even in the face of terrible adversity, our tenacity can propel us to extraordinary heights.

You might be thinking, "How can I improve my resilience?" The solution lies in adjusting your perspective. Instead of perceiving setbacks as failures, consider them chances for progress. Ask yourself, "What can I learn from this experience?" When you reframe obstacles this way, you gain a robust attitude that will help you thrive.

Unlocking your strength requires self-care.

As a parent, you may feel as if you're continuously giving to others—your child, your partner, your career, etc. It's straightforward to forget about self-care throughout the process. However, the truth is that exhaustion prevents you from accessing your inner power. Self-care is key for developing that inner strength.

Self-care is more than simply taking bubble baths or taking periodic breaks; it's about scheduling time for activities that replenish you physically, intellectually, and emotionally. This might include getting adequate sleep, eating nutritious meals, establishing appropriate boundaries, or creating time for a passion or interest. Prioritizing your personal well-being establishes a foundation for your inner power to show through.

For example, suppose you're feeling overwhelmed by your parental responsibilities. You've been exhausting yourself for several days, and it's beginning to manifest. Taking even a little break—a walk around the block or a few quiet minutes to yourself—can help you refocus your energy and perspective. You'll be astonished by how a brief period of self-replenishment can revitalize your energy and enable you to tackle challenges with renewed focus and patience.

Release negative self-talk and accept positive affirmations.

One of the most significant impediments to realizing your inner strength is negative self-talk. We all have an inner critic that tells us we aren't talented enough, we aren't strong enough, or we will never be able to overcome the obstacles we confront. But here's the reality: such notions are not true. They are merely the results of fear, uncertainty, and insecurity.

You have the capacity to alter the story in your thoughts. Positive affirmations are an effective technique for changing your mentality and accessing your inner strength. Instead of concentrating on your limitations, consider what you are capable of accomplishing. Start saying things like "I am capable," "I have the strength to handle this," or "I am doing my best, and that is enough."

According to research, positive self-talk can boost performance, reduce stress, and build resilience. So, the next time you start doubting yourself, replace those negative ideas with affirmations that remind you of your genuine strength. It may seem uncomfortable at first, but with repetition, it will become second nature.

Taking Small Steps toward Big Change

You don't need to make significant changes in your life to discover and utilize your inner power. In fact, taking tiny, regular actions is the most effective method to unleash your potential. It's common to feel overwhelmed when we consider the big picture, but if you focus on making tiny changes—day by day, minute by minute—you'll begin to see enormous benefits.

For example, instead of striving for perfection in parenting, create small, attainable objectives to help you feel more connected and in charge. Perhaps that means concentrating on one positive change at a time, such as practicing mindfulness, establishing a calmer home atmosphere, or setting aside time for yourself each day. As you succeed in these little areas, your inner power will automatically increase.

<u>Trust yourself and your instincts.</u>

You already understand what is best for you and your family. While it's straightforward to rely on the advice or opinions of others, remember that you are the expert on your own situation. Trusting yourself and your intuition is an important aspect of uncovering your inner strength.

This doesn't mean rejecting advice, but making family-friendly decisions. Trust in yourself to handle the ups and downs of motherhood and life's problems. You are strong enough to face anything that comes your way, and you know what is best for your own circumstance.

You're stronger than you believe. You already possess inner strength, just waiting to unlock it. You may access this strength by embracing resilience, practicing self-care, altering your mentality, and following your intuition. Continue your journey knowing you have enough power. All you need to do is trust in it and yourself.

Key Takeaways from Chapter 4: Self-Care and Community Development

1. Recognize Your Inner Power.

For example, Dwayne "The Rock" Johnson transformed his life from profound melancholy to global fame by embracing an inner power he didn't realize he possessed. In times of need, we all possess the same strength.

2. Building Resilience via Setbacks

Malala Yousafzai's resiliency following an assassination attempt exemplifies how hardship can feed strength. Resilience allows us to recover from setbacks and utilize them as stepping stones toward personal progress.

3. Prioritizing self-care to unlock your strengths.

The primary quote: "You can't tap into your inner strength if you're running on empty."

For example, taking a little break during a stressful day—such as a quick walk or a few minutes of deep breathing—can assist in restoring your energy and accessing your strength when obstacles come.

4. Transforming negative self-talk into positive affirmations

The primary quote: "Positive self-talk can improve

performance, reduce stress, and increase resilience."

For instance, changing thoughts like "I'm overwhelmed" to "I am capable" might change how you approach challenges and enable you to access your inner strength in commonplace circumstances.

5. Taking small, consistent steps toward large change

Setting tiny, attainable objectives, such as concentrating on one positive adjustment in your parenting or self-care routine, may result in major personal growth and help you tap into your inner power over time.

6. Trust yourself and your instincts.

For example, trusting your intuition in parenting decisions, such as discipline, boundary setting, and self-care, guarantees that you remain loyal to your inner knowledge and strength.

In Chapter 5, we'll look at how to construct a household that values respect, trust, and harmony. Just as tapping into your inner strength empowers you, building respect within your family strengthens bonds and lays the groundwork for a more caring, supportive atmosphere. Let's look at how you can foster respect and raise a successful family..

Chapter 5: Create a Home Filled with Respect and Harmony

"The difference between a successful family and one that struggles is not the absence of challenges, but the presence of confident, thoughtful solutions." - Stephen Covey

WANT YOUR CHILD TO RESPECT YOU? HERE'S HOW.

It's a common scenario: you ask your child to do something, such as finish schoolwork or pick up their toys, and they give you a look of defiance. It seems like you've asked for the impossible. You're frustrated, so are they, and everyone starts shouting. This incident does not occur once; it becomes a pattern. But what if I told you that the answer to breaking this loop isn't raising your voice or imposing stricter rules? It is about developing a culture of mutual respect. I'm talking about gaining your child's respect by demonstrating empathy, consistency, and modeling the behaviors you want to see in them.

A story that immediately comes to mind is about Sarah, a single mother I had the pleasure of working with. Sarah had been dealing with her pre-teen daughter, Olivia. No matter how many times Sarah requested Olivia to do simple chores or follow directions, Olivia would either ignore her or make a nasty remark. Sarah had run out of ideas. She had tried every type of punishment—grounding, deprivation of privileges, even threats of not being able to hang out with friends. None of it worked. In fact, it exacerbated their conflict. Sarah said, "Why isn't she listening to me anymore?" What is the answer? It was not only about authority; it was also about connection. Sarah believed that one should demand respect instead of cultivating it.

This is where most parents go wrong. We frequently believe that respect stems from our status as the adult or authoritative figure in the household. However, you cannot simply demand respect; you must earn it. Being respectful to your child builds trust, which is respect. Although you are the parent, it doesn't mean you should disregard your child's views, feelings, and opinions.

1. Set boundaries and stick to them consistently.

When it comes to developing respect, consistency is one of the most effective weapons in your parenting toolbox. Expectations help your child understand that you mean what you say. Instead of being strict or inflexible, set clear and consistent limits. Imagine if Sarah had been more consistent with her rules—if Olivia understood what would happen if she didn't listen to her mother, her conduct would most likely have altered.

Your family may have one or two essential rules. These

might include being on time for family meals, not speaking disrespectfully to others, or assisting with home duties. The trick is to apply them consistently, every day. When your kid breaches a rule, there should be an immediate, calm, and consistent consequence—something that shows them you are serious about preserving respect in the house.

Not harsh or punishing, consistency is about providing a secure environment where your child understands that your love and care have expectations. You're not only creating boundaries for the purpose of control; you're also teaching kids the value of responsibility and accountability.

2. Model Respectful Behavior for Yourself.

Has anyone heard "Children follow what you do, not what you say"? It's a reality that rings true when it comes to winning respect. You must show kindness and respect to your child. Respect is contagious; it begins with you.

Take time to consider how you communicate with your child. Are you speaking to them with compassion, or do you occasionally speak to them in impatience or irritation? It's simple to forget that our children are always seeing us and learning from how we handle stress, relationships, and communication. If kids observe you handling stressful situations with grace and empathy, they are more inclined to emulate such habits. If you are quick to lose your anger or speak rudely, kids will follow suit.

Here is one example. Assume you've had a long day at work and your youngster has forgotten to do their tasks. Instead of snapping, try saying something like, "I understand you might have forgotten, but I need you to take responsibility for the tasks we agreed on." This teaches your child that handling mistakes with respect and maturity is acceptable.

3. Listen and validate their feelings.

One of the most crucial components of developing respect with your child is demonstrating that you understand and respect their emotions. It's tempting to discount a child's feelings, especially when they're having a meltdown about something that seems insignificant to us. However, this dismissal weakens their feeling of value, making them feel disregarded and irrelevant.

Listening does not imply agreeing with everything people say; rather, it involves validating their emotions. When your child becomes unhappy, take the time to listen without interrupting. Acknowledge their emotions. You may remark, "I realize you're quite frustrated right now, and I understand why. Let's take a big breath together and discuss what's going on.

By validating your child's feelings, you demonstrate that their emotions are important, which builds reciprocal respect. Your child will respect you for caring about their emotional well-being, which will strengthen your relationship. When people feel heard, they are more inclined to appreciate you back.

4. Give them opportunities to make choices.

Empowering your child is one of the most effective ways to instill respect. Children, especially older ones, need to feel in control. Allowing kids to make decisions about their everyday activities helps them feel recognized as individuals while also teaching them responsibility.

This might begin with tiny decisions. For example, instead of instructing your child what to wear, give them a choice between two clothes. Ask them what they want to eat for dinner instead of telling them. Giving kids these options makes them feel that their opinions matter and shows respect for you, as you're not treating them like idiots.

As your child grows, you may offer them more important decisions to make. For example, you may include children in choices regarding family activities, household management, and even their own schooling. This does not imply giving up authority but rather acknowledging that your child has meaningful feedback to contribute, which leads to a deeper, more respectful connection.

5. Be Firm But Loving.

While consistency and setting limits are necessary, it's also critical to be firm while remaining warm and kind. Children must understand that your standards are non-negotiable but that you are always available to help.

For example, if your child refuses to do their homework and attempts to fight, it's crucial to be strong and say, "You need to finish your homework before you can watch TV."

While encouraging them, say you believe in them and want to help. "I understand this is difficult, but I believe in you. You can do it, and I'm available if you need assistance."

Being tough creates authority, but expressing love and support prevents your child from feeling penalized for making errors. A comfortable relationship with your child will increase their respect for you.

Finally, respect is a continuous process that involves communication, consistency, and understanding. When you focus on establishing a foundation of respect via deeds rather than simply words, your child will feel cherished and understood. Your love, guidance, and caring will earn you respect, not demand it.

Dr. Maya Angelou's renowned adage states, "People will forget what you said, what you did, but they will never forget how you made them feel." This is true for your connection with your child. The most effective tool for developing a meaningful, long-term connection based on mutual regard is the way you make people feel—respected, loved, and understood.

Discipline Without Fear: Teaching Positive Behaviors That Last

Let me tell you a tale about one of my clients named Amanda. She was a mother of two children under the age of ten. Amanda contacted me because she was fatigued. She felt like she was continuously punishing her children: taking away their toys, grounding them, and shouting at them when they misbehaved. But, despite the discipline, nothing seemed to stick. Once she stopped punishing her children, they would revert to their old habits, perpetuating the cycle. Amanda's fury was evident. "Why isn't this working? Why do they keep making the same mistakes?" she blurted out.

The issue wasn't that her children were "bad" or lacked a sense of right and wrong. The issue stemmed from the implementation of a fear-based discipline approach. Fear-based punishment may temporarily compel children to obey, but it fails to instill the behavior in them. They are merely reacting to the outcome, rather than a deeper grasp of what is beneficial and why it matters.

Discipline without fear is about creating an environment conducive to learning rather than punishing. It focuses on teaching children the principles of respect, responsibility, and empathy via positive reinforcement, clear limits, and continuous direction. And what's the beauty of this approach? It doesn't only improve behavior in the short term; it lays the groundwork for permanent beneficial behaviors and emotional development.

1. Switch from Punishment to Teaching Moments

When you think about discipline, what comes to mind? Many people face a mix of repercussions, such as timeouts, grounding, or the loss of privileges. People often perceive these strategies as the only ways to prevent negative conduct. However, teaching rather than inciting fear leads to true discipline, the type that lasts.

Consider this: when your child misbehaves, what are they actually showing you? It is not disobedience for the sake of being difficult; rather, it is a symptom that they are confused, disturbed, or unsure how to behave in a specific scenario. A youngster having a tantrum is not always a terrible child; they are simply attempting to navigate their emotions and demands.

Let's imagine your youngster is upset because he or she did not get dessert before supper. Instead of reacting in wrath or irritation, explain why dessert comes after dinner. Use the opportunity to educate kids about patience, positive habits, and the value of structure in life. You may reply, "I realize you're craving something sweet, but eating a balanced meal first will make your body feel better. And after supper, you may have your pleasure.

You see, by shifting the focus from a fight to a teaching opportunity, you are guiding your youngster toward comprehension rather than acquiescence. You are establishing the framework for kids to absorb positive behaviors rather than simply avoiding punishment. Over time, kids will naturally start making better decisions without any instruction.

<u>2. Use positive reinforcement to encourage beneficial behavior.</u>

Good reinforcement is the most effective method for teaching positive habits. The technique promotes desired behaviors rather than undesirable ones. But here's the trick: Positive reinforcement works best when it's specific, genuine, and timely.

Instead of just saying, "Good job," try to be more precise when your child accomplishes something properly. "I appreciate your selfless assistance in picking up the toys." This indicates your level of responsibility and care. This level of precision emphasizes precisely what you want to see: responsibility and care. It's no longer just about encouraging excellent conduct in general; it's also about bringing to your child's attention the outstanding qualities that you respect.

The goal is to include positive reinforcements in

everyday life. Look for opportunities throughout the day to congratulate your youngster for making the correct decision. Rather than rewarding them for every beneficial decision, this means acknowledging their beneficial decisions. Over time, your kid will begin to recognize the benefits of making excellent decisions, not for incentives, but because they are proud of their activities.

For instance, acknowledge your child's selfless assistance to a sibling. You may add, "I really appreciate how you helped your brother with his homework." That demonstrates excellent collaboration and goodwill." This simple appreciation promotes the importance of cooperation and fosters a strong emotional bond between brothers.

3. Set clear expectations and boundaries.

Setting clear, age-appropriate expectations and boundaries is an essential component of fearless discipline. Children feel safer when they comprehend the expectations and the consequences of not meeting them. Understanding the boundaries and ensuring fair and consistent responses to their activities fosters security.

Consider this: If you frequently change the rules or make them unclear, your child will get confused or frustrated. The uneven limits will leave them unsure of what to do. However, by explicitly clarifying rules like "No screen time until you finish your homework" or "We always clean up after dinner," your child gains a clear understanding of expectations and their importance. The more explicit and constant the limits, the easier it will be for your child to make decisions that meet those expectations.

Here is a simple example. Instead of saying, "Quit being so loud!""When your child is playing, give a precise expectation: "It's time to be quiet now because we need to get ready for bed." Providing them with clear instructions helps them grasp the desired behavior and why it's necessary. It also eliminates uncertainty, which can lead to dissatisfaction for both parties involved.

Consistency is essential. Fair and consistent enforcement of regulations increases the likelihood of your child obeying them, as they understand your intentions. Because they realize there's no point in pushing the limits, they'll accept them. It's not about being tough; it's about making your child feel comfortable inside the system you've established.

4. Teach empathy and responsibility.

Discipline without fear also entails teaching your child empathy—the ability to comprehend and share the emotions of others. Respect and emotional intelligence play an important role here. When a youngster can empathize with how their actions influence others, they start to comprehend the value of making responsible decisions.

One technique to develop empathy is to include your child in dispute resolution. Instead of merely penalizing your child for assaulting a sibling, ask them how they believe the sibling feels. Encourage children to express their feelings and explain the consequences of their behavior. You may reply, "I understand your anger, but punching is not the best way to cope with it. How do you believe your brother felt when you hit him?"

This technique helps your youngster develop empathy, which leads to more responsibility. It shows kids that their actions affect themselves and others. This is the essence of fearless discipline: helping your child develop an internal moral compass that guides their conduct rather than relying solely on external consequences.

5. Create an environment of trust and open communication.

Discipline works best with a solid foundation of trust and open communication. When your child understands that they can come to you with their issues, worries, and questions, they are less likely to act out in fear of punishment. Individuals will feel secure in the knowledge that you respect their thoughts and ideas.

Make it a priority to schedule regular discussions. Talk to your child about their day, what made them happy, what annoyed them, and family rules. The more openly you communicate with your child, the more likely they will trust you and feel comfortable sharing their opinions. This openness generates a sense of respect since it demonstrates that you care about their thoughts and feelings.

Open communication and mutual understanding form the foundation of discipline, making it seem less like a struggle. Instead, it is a method of navigating obstacles together. Your child will learn that making errors is a normal part of growing up and that the objective is to develop, learn, and make better decisions rather than avoid punishment.

Disciplining without fear entails more than simply persuading your youngster to comply. It's about establishing an environment in which respect, empathy, and responsibility grow organically. By concentrating on educating, reinforcing positive behavior, providing clear expectations, and fostering open communication, you provide the groundwork for long-term positive change. As your kid learns to make better decisions based on knowledge and emotional growth rather than fear, you will see a shift in behavior that will persist throughout adulthood.

As the eminent psychologist Dr. Jane Nelsen once remarked, "Children do better when they feel better." Addressing punishment with compassion and understanding will automatically improve your child's conduct, fostering a more harmonious and respected family environment.

RAISE RESILIENT CHILDREN AND FORM STRONGER FAMILIES TOGETHER.

I would like to begin with a story about a friend of mine, Emily, who faced a similar situation. Emily's daughter, Mia, was experiencing bullying at school, and she was unsure of how to assist her. Mia would come home in tears virtually every day, feeling defeated and ashamed by the children who mocked her. Emily, as a mother, felt as if she had done everything: talking to the instructors, reassuring her, and even urging her to ignore the bullies. Nonetheless, Mia's confidence continued to sink. Emily felt powerless, as if she couldn't provide the strength her daughter required.

This scenario is all too familiar to many parents. Seeing a youngster in pain or coping with a difficult situation—whether it's bullying, academic stress, or another challenge—can be daunting. You want to protect them, but you also want them to be strong enough to face life's challenges. But how can you accomplish both? How do you strengthen your child's resilience while yet being the caring parent they require?

Raising resilient children is more than simply teaching them how to deal with difficulties; it is also about creating an atmosphere in which they feel empowered to develop, adapt, and face adversity with strength and confidence. As a parent, you have an important role to play in this process. As you guide your child through each challenge, they learn from you. Your reactions to life's hardships teach children how to deal with their own.

1. Teach them to embrace mistakes as opportunities for growth.

One of the most important aspects of resilience is the capacity to see difficulties, mistakes, and failures as chances for progress. However, the challenge lies in the fact that children may not always perceive things in this manner, particularly if they haven't received instruction on how to handle failure.

Consider this: how do you respond when you make an error? Do you beat yourself up? Or do you view it as a learning opportunity and move on? Children learn from your emotions. If kids witness you being too critical of yourself or hiding your flaws, they are likely to adopt the same behavior.

Take a moment to consider a recent mistake your child committed. Perhaps they failed an exam, dropped a drink, or did not complete a job on time. How did you reply? Did you become frustrated, or did you utilize it as a learning opportunity? Rather than comforting your child after a mistake, guide them. For example, if they fail a test, rather than just reassuring them, "It's okay, you'll do better next time," ask them what they believe they might have done differently. Did they study sufficiently? Were there any techniques that they missed? Make them realize that mistakes are inevitable and an opportunity to learn and grow.

For example, if Mia made a mistake in class or misbehaved, Emily may utilize the circumstance to teach Mia how to deal with adversity productively rather than punishing her. "It is okay to be sad about this circumstance, Mia. What do you believe we should do next time to manage it better?"

This method teaches your child that mistakes are inevitable. These mistakes are simply stages on the path to mastery. Every time they make a mistake, they have the opportunity to improve and gain confidence.

2. Model resilience in your own life.

Children learn resilience by watching you, not by reading about it. If you talk all day about handling problems with strength but don't act on it, they won't take you seriously. Children observe everything you do. They witness how you deal with stress, disappointment, and frustration.

This requires you to set an example. Consider how you manage obstacles in your own life. Do you become agitated and anxious, or do you take a step back, analyze the problem, and seek a solution? When things don't go as planned, do you persevere or give up? Your children are watching—and learning how to react depending on your actions.

For example, when Emily faced a personal challenge—such as a difficult job scenario or a financial issue—she might demonstrate resilience for Mia by talking about the situation calmly and working together to solve the problem. "I realize this is difficult, but I'm going to keep trying. I will not let this setback deter me. "We will figure it out."

When you experience failures, your child should witness you handle them with kindness, tenacity, and hope. By demonstrating that difficulties are a normal part of life and can be conquered, you provide your kid the tools they need to develop their own resilience.

3. Teach coping skills for stress and anxiety.

While we can't always protect our kids from stress, we can teach them how to handle it. Daily challenges can bring us down, but resilience is more than just recovering from failure. These include school-related demands, peer disputes, and emotional upheaval.

So, how can you educate your child to manage stress and anxiety in a healthy way? One helpful strategy is to teach children mindfulness and relaxation exercises. Encourage them to take deep breaths if they feel overwhelmed or nervous. Help them identify their feelings, as this can often help them understand what they're feeling and why.

For example, if Mia is upset about a school assignment, Emily may respond, "I see you're concerned about your project. Let's take some deep breaths together. When you feel more relaxed, we can break the work down into smaller, more manageable parts." This not only soothes Mia but also teaches her that she can control her stress.

Problem-solving is another way to teach resilience. It is natural for a youngster experiencing overwhelm to want to fix everything for them. But part of parenting resilient children is helping them develop problem-solving abilities. When they face a problem, instead of instantly proposing a solution, ask them what they believe will assist. Empowering your child to think critically and solve issues boosts their confidence and allows them to deal with stress independently.

4. Foster strong relationships inside the family.

Fostering healthy, supportive family ties is one of the most effective ways to improve resilience. A strong family foundation gives the emotional security and support that children require while encountering difficulties. They need to know that they are not alone and that their family will always support them.

To lay this foundation, it's critical to spend quality time together, share experiences, and speak honestly. Family meals, game evenings, or simply sitting down to chat at the end of the day may all provide opportunities for connection. These times allow family members to better understand one another and offer emotional support as required.

When Emily and Mia were dealing with bullying, Emily made an extra effort to spend time with Mia at home, listening to her concerns, validating her feelings, and providing comfort. This made Mia feel more supported, which increased her emotional resilience. It provided her the confidence to confront her educational obstacles, knowing she had her family's support.

Furthermore, providing a supportive family environment entails more than just comforting your child when they are depressed; it also entails fostering a culture of respect, care, and love. Building your family on these ideals makes it easier for each member to face life's challenges without feeling alienated or unsupported.

5. Encourage independence and self-advocacy.

Resilient children not only overcome obstacles, but they also learn to advocate for themselves and their needs. Encourage your child to stand up for themselves, communicate their emotions, and seek support when necessary. This boosts confidence and gives them the ability to tackle challenging situations on their own.

For instance, Emily might suggest that Mia seek help from a teacher or counselor instead of intervening. "Mia, I understand how difficult this situation is. I think talking to your teacher about your feelings would help. "You deserve to feel safe at school."

Teaching your child to advocate for themselves helps them build resilience. They learn how to handle difficult circumstances by utilizing their voices, requesting assistance, and advocating for what they need.

Raising resilient children is about more than simply overcoming hardship; it is about teaching them that life's obstacles are chances for progress. It's about educating children to accept errors, demonstrating resilience in your own life, providing stress-management tools, cultivating a supportive family atmosphere, and encouraging independence. This way of raising kids teaches them how to overcome obstacles and gives them the tools they need to grow as individuals and as members of a strong, supportive family.

As the famous psychologist Dr. Susan David once said, "Resilience is not about avoiding stress but about learning how to bend, not break, when faced with life's inevitable challenges." This mindset will enable your children to face the future with confidence, knowing they have the strength to deal with whatever comes their way.

Summary of Chapter 5: Create a Home Full of Respect and Harmony

1. Do you want your child to show you respect? Here's how.

Key Point: Mutual respect is the core of family relationships; your respect for your child generates respect in return.

Emily taught Mia to accept boundaries by recognizing

her own needs and limitations. Mia learned to give herself room when she needed it and to listen to her problems, which she then applied to other people.

<u>2. Discipline Without Fear: Teaching Positive Behaviors That Last</u>

Key Point: Discipline based on love and compassion, rather than fear, is the key to instilling enduring behavioral change in children.

Instead of punishing Mia when she misbehaved, Emily held calm chats with her, assisting Mia in understanding the repercussions of her behavior and encouraging her toward better decisions.

<u>3. Raise resilient children and form stronger families together.</u>

Key Point: Consistent family support fosters resilience, errors are encouraged as learning opportunities, and children are taught to tackle obstacles with fortitude.

For instance, Emily showed resilience in the face of Mia's bullying by working through their problems as a family, demonstrating their ability to overcome hardship.

As we conclude Chapter 5, in which we established the foundations for establishing a respectful household, it is time to shift our emphasis. Chapter 6 will look at how to apply these ideas to real-world situations. How do you approach the chaos of morning rituals, the stress of schoolwork, and the difficulties of family dynamics with confidence and ease?

Chapter 6: Tackle Everyday Challenges with Confidence

"The difference between a successful family and one that struggles is not the absence of challenges, but the presence of confident, thoughtful solutions." - Stephen Covey

CHALLENGE DAY ONE: MORNING CHAOS? LET US MAKE YOUR ROUTINES SMOOTHER.

Mornings can be crazy, right? You're not alone if your morning routine feels more like a conflict than a peaceful beginning to the day. If your morning ritual feels more like a war than a tranquil start to the day, you're not alone. But what if we could fix this? What if you could begin each day with a sense of peace and control, rather than turmoil and frustration?

Let's take a deep breath together, because what we're going to do is simple—but effective. I'm not suggesting you wake up at 4:30 a.m., meditate for an hour, or completely organize your life. No. We'll concentrate on practical, concrete techniques to make your mornings easier. So let's get started.

<u>Step 1: The Night Before—Set the Stage for Success</u>

I know what you're thinking: "How in the world can I prepare for the morning the night before? I'm barely holding it together as it is!" But bear with me here. One of the simplest ways to alleviate the stress of a hectic morning is to plan ahead of time. If you can make little changes the night before, it will make all the difference.

Here's the first practical thing I want you to accomplish tonight: lay out everyone's clothes. This one step can save you about 15 minutes of decision-making in the morning. You probably already know the routine: one child wants to wear yesterday's outfit, while the other prefers an unlikely match. So, instead of tackling the mess when you're already running late, prepare your clothes the night before. For children, it's an excellent chance to include them in decision-making while also instilling responsibility.

For instance, my friend Laura initiated the practice of arranging her children's clothing the night before, resulting in significant improvements. There were no more last-minute questions like "Where is my favorite shirt?" or "I don't want to wear that!" The youngsters were already prepared and confident in their decisions. This simplified her decision-making process and ensured a smooth morning.

Step 2: Create a morning checklist.

Now that you've established the context, let's discuss how to simplify the morning itself. One of the most common complaints among parents is that the morning is chaotic. Kids forget things, the to-do list is onerous, and time simply slips away. This is when a basic checklist comes in useful.

A morning checklist keeps everyone on track, including you and your youngster. It's easy, visually appealing, and an excellent method to relieve tension. You don't have to make things complicated; simply focus on the fundamentals. Consider it a treasure map: each activity represents a milestone that brings you closer to the "X," where the school bus awaits.

For example, you could create a morning checklist with the following items:

- Wake up and get dressed.
- Eat breakfast.
- Brush teeth.
- Pack the backpack.
- Put shoes on.
- Get out the door!
- Check the weather (to determine if you need an umbrella or a jacket).

You may make this checklist more appealing to younger children by using images. For older children, a basic list is adequate. Place it on the refrigerator or anywhere they can see it. This gives them ownership of the process—and, more crucially, it allows you to stay organized and focused.

For example, my cousin Sarah created a checklist for her first-grade daughter, Emily. It was simple and bright, and Emily enjoyed ticking off each duty as she did it. What was the result? Sarah's mornings transitioned from hectic and frustrated to simple and productive. Emily understood what to do next, and Sarah didn't have to continuously remind her.

Step 3: Create a "Buffer Zone" for Extra Time.

We've all been there: something goes wrong, and you find yourself running late. The fact is that things do not always go as planned. Your child might accidentally spill juice on their shirt, or someone might take too long to brush their teeth. This is where a "buffer zone" comes in. Allow yourself 10–15 extra minutes in the morning in case things do not go as planned.

When you have this cushion, it relieves pressure. If you're always striving to squeeze every last minute out of your morning, even the tiniest setback feels terrible. However, if you've included a buffer, you'll find it easier to remain cool when things don't go as planned. Furthermore, you won't be racing about like a crazy person, resulting in a less stressful start for everyone concerned.

For example, when my neighbor, Jessie, began introducing a buffer zone into her daily routine, she discovered that she could deal with the typical morning hiccups without worry. If someone spilled milk or couldn't locate their schoolwork, she didn't stress since she had more time. She no longer had to rush to the car, and the children felt less stressed.

Step 4: Establish a "No Tech" zone before school.

This task can be challenging, particularly in today's environment where everyone is engrossed in their devices. But trust me when I say that avoiding screens during the first hour of the morning will help everyone focus. Phones, tablets, and even the television may be a major distraction. You want your family to be present and focused on the most essential portion of the morning: preparing for the day ahead.

Establish a rule prohibiting the use of phones or screens for the first 30-45 minutes after waking up. Use that time to have breakfast, get dressed, and complete any necessary morning duties. Distracted by phones in the morning, you or your kids will move slower and create more tension.

Tina, a friend of mine, has adopted a no-screen rule for her children in the mornings. They protested it at first, but Tina quickly saw something incredible: the kids were getting dressed faster, with fewer distractions, and they were much more interested in talks with her throughout breakfast. The mornings became more quiet and orderly.

Step 5: Concentrate on a calm start, not a hectic sprint.

Here's an often-overlooked fact: how you start your morning sets the tone for the rest of the day. If you start with worry and turmoil, your family will carry that throughout the day. On the other side, if you establish a peaceful tone in the morning, you'll be surprised at how much easier things go.

Here's where it gets practical: start each morning with a brief, relaxing exercise. This may be as simple as a few minutes of breathing exercises, stretching, or even a brief family embrace. It doesn't have to be a lengthy ritual; just enough to anchor you and transfer your attention from frenzied energy to quiet production.

For example, my friend Michelle began getting up 10 minutes earlier to do a little meditation with her children.

They would sit on the couch together, take deep breaths, and relax their thoughts. This allowed Michelle, who was previously harried and angry, to begin her day feeling more centered. The kids followed her lead, and the morning routine evolved into one that focused on bonding before the day began rather than racing.

Step 6: Make breakfast simple yet healthy.

Finally, breakfast. To maintain energy, attention, and well-being, it doesn't have to be a challenging meal. The objective is to provide a quick, easy, and healthy breakfast that will nourish everyone for the day ahead without adding unnecessary stress.

If you struggle with mornings and frequently skip breakfast or eat sugary cereals, it's time to reconsider your options. You can prepare healthy breakfast alternatives the night before or keep quick snacks like yogurt, granola bars, or fruit on hand. The idea is to have a few healthy and easily accessible selections.

For example, Katie discovered that preparing breakfast the night before, such as overnight oats or smoothie packs ready to combine, made mornings go much more smoothly. Her children were not hurrying to prepare breakfast, and they ate something nutritious that provided them energy to go through the school day.

So, let's go over everything we learned today. The key to better mornings is to make incremental, regular modifications rather than big changes. Lay out clothing the night before. Challenge Day One: Morning Chaos? Let us make your routines smoother.

Mornings can be crazy, right? You're not alone if your morning routine feels more like a conflict than a peaceful beginning to the day. If your morning ritual feels more like a war than a tranquil start to the day, you're not alone. But what if we could fix this? What if you could begin each day with a sense of peace and control, rather than turmoil and frustration?

Let's take a deep breath together, because what we're going to do is simple—but effective. I'm not suggesting you wake up at 4:30 a.m., meditate for an hour, or completely organize your life. No. We'll concentrate on practical, concrete techniques to make your mornings easier. So let's get started.

Challenge Day 2: Are you stressed about your homework? Turn it into a team effort.

Let's be honest, schoolwork may seem like a fight. You know the scenario: your child returns home with a bag full of schoolwork, and the instant they open that folder, the air thickens with stress. You're looking at the clock, counting down the minutes till supper, and wondering how you're going to get through the mountain of duties ahead of you. Stress intensifies, tensions escalate, and what once seemed like a productive hour transforms into a turbulent emotional journey.

Let me tell you a way to make schoolwork fun and manageable. Instead of adding to the stress, how about demonstrating to your child that learning is not a solo endeavor? This is where the story shifts from dissatisfaction to partnership. It's time to make homework a collaborative activity that fosters resilience, encourages positive habits, and ensures everyone feels supported.

Step 1: Establish a homework-friendly environment.

Imagine your youngster sitting at the kitchen table, books open and papers scattered everywhere. The strain in the air is palpable. What is lacking from the scene? The correct atmosphere. Homework, like any other endeavor, needs a conducive environment for concentration and production.

Begin by establishing a distinct "homework zone" devoid of distractions. It should not be a separate room but rather a place where your child can sit and concentrate. This area should be well organized, with all required materials, such as pencils, erasers, and paper, easily accessible. A messy, disorganized environment might make homework seem burdensome before it even starts.

Also, consider lighting. Bright lighting may keep your youngster attentive and focused, but low or inadequate lighting might cause weariness. Make sure the environment is quiet enough for focus but not too secluded to cause emotions of loneliness.

For example, my friend Lisa turned her kitchen nook into a pleasant homework center for her children. She included a tiny workstation, a comfy chair, and a few colorful storage boxes for supplies. Her children adored the room since it provided them with their own private spot to relax and work. Homework became less stressful and more productive since they had a dedicated location to focus.

Step 2: Establish a Routine (Same Time, Same Place)

A schedule is an effective tool, and consistency is especially important when it comes to homework. You need a consistent homework regimen, just as you do in the mornings. Setting aside time each day for homework helps your child realize that it is a necessary part of the day, just like cleaning their teeth or eating dinner. It establishes expectations and allows them to mentally prepare for the job ahead.

Now I understand—some days are busier than others, and it's difficult to keep to a regular plan. However, try to set a time frame, whether it's immediately after school, after a snack, or after a brief break. The aim is consistency, not rigidity. Students can complete homework without procrastination or surprise if they know.

For example, my sister, Emma, began scheduling "homework time" immediately after her children returned home from school. At 4 p.m., they realized it was time to sit down and get to work. The framework helped her children remain on track, and they eventually developed a feeling of responsibility and routine for their assignments.

Step 3: Work Together—Be an Active Participant.

Though homework may seem like just supervision, what if you could do more? Be an active participant. Instead of sitting on the sidelines, join in. Showing your involvement helps your child focus and lets them know they're not alone.

Don't simply check the answers at the end; help brainstorm, clarify difficult topics, and remain cool when frustrated. If your child is struggling with a problem, collaborate with them to solve it step-by-step. Use real-life examples to help others grasp topics. Perhaps it's a math problem related to grocery shopping or a scientific question about plants that you can connect to observations you've made in your garden.

For example, a mother I know consistently sits with her child during homework time but not in a "do it for them" manner. Instead, she asks leading questions like, "What do you think would happen if you did this?" She also asks, "Could you describe the stages in your own words?" This has helped her child gain confidence in his talents, as he knows his mother is there to encourage him rather than oversee.

Step 4: Break tasks into manageable chunks.

One of the leading causes of homework stress is the overwhelming sense of having too much to accomplish. When your child sees a stack of schoolwork, it might feel like an insurmountable challenge. That is why it is critical to divide work into tiny, achievable parts.

Start by reviewing the tasks and assisting your youngster in prioritizing them. Is there something due tomorrow? Could they prioritize completing a simpler task to boost their sense of accomplishment? Make a strategy of attack. Taking one task at a time, rather than gazing at the entire pile, will let students feel more in control and less overwhelmed.

When Steve and his son Max faced a large history assignment, they divided it into three parts: research, planning, and writing. They enthusiastically praised each step as they completed it. Max not only finished the assignment ahead of schedule, but he also felt proud of his accomplishment. Steve had helped him transform a massive assignment into a doable procedure, and the stress had vanished.

Step 5: Celebrate the Wins, No Matter How Small

Here's the thing: schoolwork may be exhausting for both you and your child. However, it doesn't have to be all about difficulty. When your youngster has completed a task, rejoice! It doesn't have to be a substantial amount of money; acknowledging their hard work could have a significant impact. A simple "Great job!" or a high-five could boost their confidence and motivate them to continue their efforts.

If it's been a particularly difficult session, why not reward them with something they enjoy? Consider rewarding them with their favorite food, some enjoyable moments, or even organizing a small dance party in the living room. Whatever works best for you and your child, the idea is to reaffirm that hard work pays dividends.

One family I know has a "homework jar." When their children accomplish an assignment, they may choose a little gift from the jar, such as a sticker, a special snack, or additional screen time. It's become a joyful part of the routine, and the kids are looking forward to finishing their schoolwork.

Step 6: Show Calmness—Your energy sets the tone.

Children are observant and may pick up on the energy

around them. If you are upset, rushed, or frustrated, your youngster will most likely imitate your behavior. That is why demonstrating serenity is essential during homework time. Take a deep breath, even if everything seems to be coming apart. Your calm demeanor will help your youngster stay focused.

When your child is struggling with an assignment, it's tempting to become frustrated. But remember, you are the role model. Show them how to maintain their composure in the face of adversity. A simple "Let's take a break and come back to it" or "This is tough, but I know you can do it" could make a significant difference. Your ability to remain composed will make them feel supported.

For instance, a father named Brian confided in me that he used to become agitated during homework time, especially when his daughter, Ella, struggled to understand anything. However, after realizing how his fury affected her, he began modeling tranquility. He'd tell her, "It's okay, we'll figure it out together," and give her space to breathe. His change of approach helped Ella remain cool, and schoolwork became less difficult for both of them.

Homework does not have to be a fight. With the correct equipment, a little forethought, and a helpful mindset, you can make it a pleasant experience for both you and your child. Remember, you're not simply supervising; you're collaborating as a team. You're developing skills, confidence, and resilience along the way. And, with time, you'll realize that homework is more than just completing tasks; it's about learning to confront obstacles together. So, let us keep the momentum continuing, because you and your child are capable of amazing things.

Challenge Day 3: End Your Day Right: Establish a Relaxing Bedtime Routine

After a long day of school, activities, and duties, it might feel like the toughest part of the day is putting your child to bed. Does your nightly routine feel like a competition against time? Perhaps your youngster resists, fights sleep, or drags out every step, leaving you both fatigued. You know you need that serene moment of relaxation, but it seems difficult to find it. If your bedtime ritual feels more like a struggle than a pleasant way to sleep, you're not alone.

But what if I told you that having a relaxing sleep ritual doesn't have to be difficult? It may be the highlight of your day—a chance to reconnect with your child and relax. It's all about creating a routine that relaxes, soothes, and prepares your child for sleep. When done correctly, it not only makes sleep easier but also improves your child's mood and conduct. And the greatest part? It can also help you get much-needed slumber.

So, let's look at ways to make sleep a calm, restful experience for both you and your child.

Step 1: Create a consistent bedtime schedule.

Helping your youngster wind down requires consistency. Having a scheduled bedtime and a consistent routine is critical for their internal clock. When toddlers understand that it is time to wind down at the same time every night, their bodies begin to anticipate sleep, allowing them to fall asleep effortlessly.

Repetition makes it easier for your child to settle in without resistance. If you've been irregular with your bedtime, don't worry—it's never too late to start. Take a mutually convenient time and stick to it. The objective is to maintain consistency rather than achieve perfection.

For example, my friend Sarah began establishing bedtime for her daughter, Lily, at 8 p.m. Every night. It didn't happen overnight, but Lily's body gradually adjusted. She knew that at 8 p.m., it was time to relax, and Sarah no longer had to follow her around the house or beg her to go to bed. That minor modification made a significant difference.

Step 2: Establish a Calming Pre-Bedtime Routine

Pre-bedtime and bedtime are equally important for your child. Rushing bedtime or causing conflict can agitate your child and hinder their ability to fall asleep. This is why sticking to a consistent pre-bedtime routine will help you fall asleep more easily.

The pre-bedtime ritual should begin 30-60 minutes before your real bedtime. This is when you slow down the evening's pace. Begin by dimming the lights to convey to your child's brain that the day is ending. Turn off all displays, including televisions, smartphones, and tablets. Screens emit blue light that disrupts the production of melatonin, the hormone responsible for regulating sleep. Instead, try relaxing activities like reading a book, having a warm bath, or listening to quiet music.

My relative, Tom, used to let his children run about until bedtime. It caused a lot of chaos, making it difficult for them to relax. However, as he established a relaxing pre-bedtime routine—dimming the lights, reading together, and spending some quiet time before brushing teeth—their conduct dramatically improved. The children began to look forward to bedtime, and the procedure became much more relaxing.

Step 3: Turn Bedtime Into a Connection Time

It's simple to forget that nighttime may be a particular opportunity to bond. After a full day of school, work, and activities, nighttime is one of the few opportunities to truly bond with your child. So make it count! Whether you spend time hugging, talking about the day, or sharing a bedtime tale, try to make this a time for connection rather than hurrying through it.

If your child is old enough, ask them about their day and listen closely. Share something wonderful that happened to you today. This promotes a sense of emotional safety and comfort. It also makes your child feel heard and understood, which helps them relax and get ready for bed.

For example, my neighbor Laura and her daughter have a nightly routine in which they each share one "happy moment" from their day before reading a tale together. It's their unique time to connect and reflect, and her daughter, Ava, is looking forward to it. They've seen that this connection time has improved Ava's sleep and made her feel more safe.

Step 4: Maintain a soothing bedroom environment.

Make your bedroom a relaxing environment. You want to establish a tranquil sleeping environment that promotes relaxation. Start by ensuring that the space is cold, dark, and silent. You may use blackout curtains to block out light and a white noise machine to muffle outdoor noises. A comfy bed and clean linens are essential for getting a satisfying night's sleep.

Consider introducing relaxing smells into the bedroom. Lavender, chamomile, and other soothing smells help alert your child's brain that it's time to sleep. To create this soothing environment before bedtime, use a diffuser, pillow spray, or scented lotion.

For example, I know a family who regularly used lavender-scented pillows and a white noise generator. Their kid was first skeptical of the notion, but after a few nights, he learned to equate the scent and sound with sleep. It became a soothing cue, allowing him to go to sleep more easily.

Step 5: Be patient with your child's sleeping needs.

It's vital to remember that every child sleeps differently. Some children require longer time to fall asleep, and some may struggle with nighttime anxiety. Be patient and allow your child the time they need to go from awake to asleep.

If your child becomes apprehensive about bedtime, attempt to console them without delaying the process. Avoid inadvertently fostering a fear of nighttime. Instead, try offering calm reassurance. If your youngster requests "one more story," set a limit and politely explain that it's time to sleep. You may also provide a tiny comfort, such as a beloved stuffed animal or blanket, to make them feel more safe.

For example, my friend Olivia used to become frustrated when her daughter, Emma, requested more tales or hugs before bedtime. However, after speaking with a sleep specialist, she learned to be patient and set moderate boundaries. She began telling Emma, "I'll give you two more minutes of cuddles, and then it's time to rest." This allowed Emma to feel comfortable without prolonging the nighttime process.

Step 6: Remain calm—Your energy sets the tone.

Your youngster looks to you for indications on how to deal with events. Your child will pick up on your hurry and concern about bedtime. Your calm demeanor sets the tone for the entire nighttime process.

When you are comfortable, your child understands that it is okay to let go of the day and rest. If your youngster is resistant, be patient and don't let irritation show. Sometimes just being there, speaking calmly, and maintaining a constant rhythm will make your child feel safe and secure.

Sarah, as previously indicated, used to become worried when her son, Max, refused to go to bed. But after some coaching on how to stay cool and regulate her own energy, she saw a significant improvement. Max began to catch up on her calm demeanor, which made him more relaxed. Their sleep routine now feels more like a tranquil ritual than a conflict.

Creating a tranquil sleep ritual requires consistency, calmness, and connection. It's about transforming sleep from a struggle into a relaxing finale to a hectic day. When you build a pattern that seems secure and relaxing, your child will sleep better, and so will you. Most importantly, it provides a chance to bond, reflect, and demonstrate to your child that their well-being is your number one concern.

So let us make tonight the beginning of something great. Take a deep breath, relax, and trust that your child is going to bed feeling safe, loved, and ready for a wonderful night's sleep. The ripple effects of these quiet evenings will lead to brighter, more peaceful days for everybody.

Challenge Day 4: Family Conflicts? Learn How to Speak Without Yelling.

Let's face it: family disputes are unavoidable. Whether it's a simple debate over what to eat for supper or a more serious one concerning chores or curfews, emotions run high, and the screaming begins. Like most parents, you've probably gone through this cycle more times than you realize. The positive news is that you don't have to continue following this pattern. Family fights do not have to end in yelling, frustration, or guilt. There is a better approach to dealing with those moments when emotions threaten to take over—and it begins with knowing how to communicate without shouting.

But here's the truth: calm, successful communication does not happen overnight. It involves focus, self-awareness, and practice. Today, I'll lead you through some practical methods to help stop the cycle of yelling and teach your family how to speak politely, even in the heat of the moment.

Step one: recognize the triggers and pause.

The first step in every disagreement is to detect when things begin to escalate. If you're ready to rant, ask yourself, "What's making me so angry?" The problem may be how your child speaks to you or your day's stress. In many cases, we react with anger to something deeper than the present.

For example, my friend Jenny noticed that anytime her kid, Lucas, did not immediately respond to her, she felt a surge of irritation. She didn't realize at first that her own work-related stress levels were impacting how she responded to his actions. Jenny realized this and was able to catch herself before snapping. She would take a deep breath, stand back, and hesitate before speaking. This little move allowed her to maintain her composure and avoid escalating matters.

Taking a minute to pause allows you to consider your reaction rather than reacting immediately. It may only take a few seconds, but you'll notice that you're more likely to make a considered, calm choice rather than allowing anger to dictate your words.

Step 2: Use "I" statements rather than "you" statements.

Using phrases like "you always..." or "you never..." may quickly put someone on the defensive. Pointing fingers at others might make them feel accused and assaulted. This often leads to their retaliation, escalating the situation. Instead, focus on how you feel about the issue.

Use "I" expressions to express your feelings without assigning blame. Instead of expressing, "You never listen to me," try, "I feel frustrated when I have to repeat myself." This softens the message and opens the way to a more constructive discourse.

For example, when my sister Emily argued with her daughter Zoe about cleaning up her room, Zoe would often roll her eyes or disregard her mother. Emily's first instinct was to shout, but she began to use "I" statements instead. She'd remark, "I'm feeling overwhelmed by all the mess and need some help." This minor adjustment helped Zoe better comprehend her mother's feelings, resulting in a more cooperative response.

The idea here is that using "I" words prevents the debate from becoming accusatory and promotes discussion instead of creating a wall of defensiveness.

Step 3: Practice active listening and empathy.

When conflicts erupt, we frequently focus on what we are going to say next rather than what the other person is attempting to express. Active listening is an effective technique for de-escalating disagreements and fostering a better understanding between you and your child.

If you disagree, active listening is hearing what the other person is saying and showing empathy. This includes putting down your phone, making eye contact, and not interrupting. Consider what you've heard and ask yourself, "So, are you upset because I didn't let you go out with your friends?" "This demonstrates that you are paying attention and are concerned about their feelings."

For example, my friend Clara used to become irritated when her teenage son, Max, argued over curfew. He would start ranting, and she would get defensive. But once she started to really listen, everything changed. Instead of interrupting, she would let Max talk before gently saying, "I realize you're unhappy. Let's find out how to make this work together." The outcome? Max felt heard, and they were able to reach the settlement without shouting.

Active listening prevents miscommunication and exhibits regard for the other person's feelings. It is a vital tool for transforming family disagreements into calm, constructive discussions.

Step 4: Maintain calm body language.

In the midst of an argument, your body language speaks much more than your words. If you stand with your arms crossed, face stiff, or voice elevated, your youngster will feel frightened or defensive. Nonverbal signs may swiftly exacerbate a situation, just like a rising voice.

When speaking to your child, make sure your body language reflects openness and calm. Uncross your arms, take deep breaths, and speak in a calm, steady tone. Your posture should indicate that you are accessible and eager to engage in a calm talk.

A number of years ago, I witnessed a dad, John, having a furious argument with his daughter, Sarah. At first, John took a firm stance and raised his voice. Then he remembered to breathe deeply and uncross his arms. He leaned in slightly to demonstrate that he was interested, and his tone softened. Sarah's body language became more calm almost instantly. She stopped yelling and began listening.

Calm body language does more than simply help you communicate more successfully; it also establishes a serene tone that helps your youngster to respond appropriately.

Step 5: Set and maintain boundaries.

You can't have a fruitful conversation when one person is shouting and the other is attempting to remain calm. Setting limits is vital for keeping the discourse civil. If shouting begins, tell your youngster calmly that it is time to take a break.

You can remark, "I realize you're furious, but we can't discuss while shouting. Let's take a few minutes and then try again." This boundary emphasizes that screaming is not appropriate and that both sides must maintain a polite discussion.

When Michelle's son, Evan, began shouting at her during their weekly chore conversation, she set a boundary. She responded, "Evan, I understand your frustration, but we need to have a calm discourse. If we keep shouting, we'll have to take a break and try again later." Evan eventually learned to respect these boundaries and began approaching talks more calmly.

Setting clear communication limits allows you to maintain respect even in tense situations. You can also calm down before the conversation turns regrettable.

Step 6: Teach problem solving together.

Finally, use family fights to teach problem-solving skills. When you remain cool and politely work through differences, you are demonstrating effective conflict resolution methods. Encourage your child to communicate their emotions and work together to find a solution. Instead of just prescribing the conclusion, engage them in the decision-making process. This prepares children to tackle difficulties productively in the future.

For instance, during dinner one evening, Mark and his daughter, Olivia, disagreed regarding Olivia's curfew. Instead of just enforcing his decision, Mark inquired, "What do you believe would be a reasonable curfew? Let's talk about it and find a solution that works for both of us." This collaborative approach not only fixed the problem but also made Olivia feel empowered and appreciated.

When you model problem-solving via calm talks, you not only defuse current disagreements, but you also teach your child how to manage conflict in the future without resorting to shouting.

Family conflicts are inevitable, but they don't have to end in commotion. Practicing these strategies—recognizing triggers, utilizing "I" statements, actively listening, keeping calm body language, setting limits, and teaching problem-solving—lays the groundwork for respectful communication in your household. With time and effort, disagreements will become chances to connect, learn, and develop together, rather than sources of stress and division.

So, the next time an argument arises, remember that you have the ability to shift the path of the debate. With patience, empathy, and these tools at your disposal, you can transform every disagreement into an opportunity for growth and understanding.

Challenge Day 5: Simple Habits for Keeping Your Family Close Every Day.

When you think about your family, what comes to mind? Is it laughing at the dinner table, peaceful times in the evening, or shared experiences that have left lasting impressions? Families build and reinforce their relationships not only during significant events but also through everyday behaviors. Today's assignment is all about discovering the simple, everyday rituals that keep your family close, connected, and emotionally supported. These may appear to be trivial details in the larger scheme of things, but they are critical to developing long-term, meaningful connections with your loved ones.

Step one: Make daily check-ins a priority.

Implementing regular check-ins is one of the easiest and most successful strategies to stay connected with your family.

A check-in does not have to be a lengthy conversation; it may simply be a minute in which you ask your child (or spouse) how they are doing. Spending just a few minutes catching up with each individual can keep your family on track.

For example, every day, my friend Lisa, a busy mother of two, finds time to sit down with each of her children, Noah and Emma, for a few minutes after school. She doesn't immediately ask them about their day. Instead, she starts by asking a simple question such as "How are you feeling today?" or "What's anything exciting that happened?" This simple ritual maintains open lines of communication and enables each family member to discuss their day according to their own preferences. It has helped their family feel closer together, and they have a greater understanding of one another's emotions.

These moments can last as little as two minutes, but they make a huge difference in terms of emotional availability and closeness. When your family realizes they can rely on these check-ins, they will be more willing to share their thoughts and feelings with you.

Step 2: Eat together as often as possible.

With our hectic lifestyles, it's simple for everyone to be in different places during mealtimes. However, shared meals are one of the most effective methods for families to bond and communicate. According to studies, families that eat together on a daily basis have greater emotional attachments, healthier communication, and overall stronger relationships.

It's not necessarily about the food—it's about spending

quality time together, free of distractions, where everyone can sit down, share their opinions, and reconnect. Whether it's breakfast, lunch, or supper, dining together allows you to bond and discuss your day.

For example, my neighbor Rachel makes it a point to have family dinners at least five evenings per week. Even if she is exhausted from work or has a hectic schedule, she prioritizes this time. She forbids anyone from using their phones at the dinner table. The family discusses the day, shares humorous stories, or discusses upcoming events. It's become a special time for them, and Rachel has observed that her children, Jake and Mia, are more forthcoming with her than ever.

Even if you don't have the luxury of sitting down for every meal together, strive to make one meal every day—breakfast, lunch, or dinner—a family event. This simple practice not only develops intimacy, but it also produces long-lasting memories that your children will treasure forever.

Step 3: Establish family traditions, big and small.

Family rituals are a wonderful method to strengthen your bond with one another. It's the traditions, both significant and little, that give your family a feeling of identity. Whether it's something as huge as an annual family vacation or something more intimate like Friday night movie marathons, these traditions generate a sense of continuity and belonging that enhances the family tie.

Traditions do not have to be complicated or expensive. They might be as basic as a unique handshake or a cherished bedtime story passed down through generations. What matters most is that you do them regularly and the whole family enjoys them.

Every Sunday morning, Sarah and her two children, Luke and Emma, prepare pancakes together. They've had this ritual since Luke was a toddler. Even as the children get older, they continue to look forward to their pancake morning. More than the pancakes, the laughing, collaboration, and shared delight create an unseen bond.

When thinking about your family, consider what tiny rituals or traditions you can start or develop. These experiences foster a strong feeling of family togetherness and serve as a continuous reminder to your children of the necessity of spending quality time together.

Step 4: Spend one-on-one time with every family member.

One of the most effective ways to keep your family together is to ensure that everyone feels seen and heard. While group activities and family time are important, spending individual time with each family member develops the special link you have with them. Your children are not a single entity; they are people with their own ideas, feelings, and wants.

It's tempting to believe that family connection stems from doing things together, but the fact is that individual attention makes each family member feel appreciated. Set aside time to engage with your child individually. Perhaps it's a stroll in the park, a trip to the library, or simply reading together before bed. Make them feel like the center of your world at that moment.

For example, Rachel has three children and began a new endeavor last year. Every week, she spends one-on-one time with each youngster. She'll take 10-year-old Leo to an ice cream store one day and 5-year-old Sophie to the park for swings the next. They don't discuss school or housework. Instead, they just chat about whatever comes to mind—often something basic, such as their favorite animals or their future goals. Rachel has discovered that these short, constant one-on-one interactions enable her to connect with each kid in a unique and personal way.

If you have more than one child, schedule individual time with them on a regular basis. Even if it's only for 15 minutes, this focused time makes them feel important and helps you to form meaningful connections.

Step 5: Display physical affection every day.

It's simple to overlook the importance of physical affection, especially when life is hectic. However, simple gestures such as hugs, high-fives, and holding hands may instill a strong sense of security and affection in a family. Physical affection does not need to be extravagant—it may be as basic as a slap on the back or a short hug before leaving for school or work.

Physical affection is essential for children's emotional development, while it strengthens sentiments of love and trust in adults. Whether it's a hug at the start of the day or a kiss on the cheek before sleep, these tiny gestures of physical contact help to foster emotional intimacy in the family.

For example, I know a family in which the mother, Marissa, begins each morning by hugging her two children, Jack and Lily, before they go to school. It's a must-do practice that has helped them feel grounded and connected. Even when the kids are unhappy or upset, this daily display of affection makes them feel cherished and prepared to face the day.

So, make it a practice to show your affection physically. Hugs, kisses, and simply a pat on the shoulder are more powerful than you may believe.

You won't remember the big events from the day. Small, constant moments are what genuinely bring a family closer together. By prioritizing daily check-ins, dining together, building family rituals, spending one-on-one time with each member, and displaying physical affection, you can cultivate a household where love, trust, and communication thrive.

So don't underestimate the power of small things. Simple behaviors, practiced on a daily basis, serve as the glue that holds your family together. When you include these behaviors into your daily routine, you foster an environment in which your family feels emotionally supported, connected, and truly loved.

It's not always necessary to do huge, extravagant things; instead, make tiny, meaningful efforts every day to show your family how much you care about them. What was the result? The outcome was a family that was stronger, more bonded, and more resilient. That is something we should strive for.

Challenge Day 6: Reflect on Your Growth: Celebrate the Progress You Have Made

Today, we've achieved a significant milestone. It's not about completing additional activities or adding to your to-do list today; instead, we're pausing. We reflect. We are pleased with the progress you have already achieved. This challenge isn't just about solving difficulties or aiming for perfection; it's also about celebrating minor triumphs along the road and recognizing how far you've gone.

In a society that is continuously going forward, it is tempting to focus on what comes next. However, it is equally vital to take a minute to reflect. Reflecting on your work provides not just a sense of success but also motivation to keep going.

Step 1: Acknowledge Small Wins.

We frequently hurry through life without giving ourselves credit for what we have already accomplished. It's tempting to believe that we haven't accomplished enough and that setting new goals is more essential than enjoying our accomplishments. But today, you're going to halt and celebrate your victories, no matter how minor they may appear.

Did you get through a crazy morning without shouting at anyone? Did you set aside time for a family supper or an uninterrupted talk with your child? Those are wins. Those are positive moves forward.

For example, my friend Anna, a mother of three, told me that even the tiniest things used to make her feel dejected. She didn't have time for a decent breakfast one morning due to the normal hurry, but she was able to sit down with her children and have a quiet talk before they went to school. She declared this a victory. Not the whole morning, just one peaceful moment when they bonded. And it matters. By seeing it as a success, she reinforced the concept that it's not always about having the ideal day—it's about the moments that remind you of what actually counts.

Take a moment to mention your personal accomplishments. Don't underestimate them, no matter how little they appear. Each is a success, and acknowledging them amplifies their impact.

Step 2: Reflect on your challenges and what you have learned.

Reflection involves discovering what went wrong as well as celebrating what went right. Every struggle and failure provides a chance for progress. Perhaps you have battled with consistency or found yourself reverting to old patterns. That is okay. You've still learned something useful in the process.

Think of times when you were frustrated and wanted to give up. What have you learned from those experiences? You may have learned about self-compassion or how to better manage your triggers. Growth doesn't always happen in a linear fashion. It's sloppy and flawed, but it's still growing.

Take Emily, for example. Throughout her children's tantrums, Emily has maintained her composure, yet there were moments when her patience wavered. Instead of beating herself up, she thought on previous experiences and concluded she needed better techniques for dealing with stress in the moment. She started by practicing deep breathing and incorporating small, soothing routines into her daily routine. These setbacks were not failures; rather, they provided possibilities for improvement.

Think about your own issues. What did you learn? Reflecting on these experiences makes you stronger, more resilient, and more confident in your capacity to deal with whatever comes your way.

Step 3: Monitor your progress over time.

When you track your progress, you can frequently see it more clearly. It's easy to lose sight of your progress when immersed in the rat race. Keeping a basic notebook, recording your objectives, or even taking daily notes on how you feel will allow you to monitor your progress in real time.

Set aside time today to reflect on the preceding week or

month. What is different today than when you started? Has your capacity to remain cool under difficult situations improved? Is your family meal more relaxed? Do you feel closer to your children? Tracking your progress allows you to see what you've done and reminds you that change takes time.

For example, John, the father of two, keeps a notebook in which he records his daily successes, frustrations, and overall sentiments. When he looks back at his entries from the previous month, he observes that his patience has improved, and he can now remain calm in difficult situations for longer periods of time. He didn't regularly consider this, but after reviewing his notebook, it became glaringly obvious.

Begin charting your progress, whether in a basic notebook or on your phone. Write down your minor victories, problems, and everything in between. You'll be surprised by how much you've done.

Step 4: Share your successes with others.

Sometimes we need to hear people acknowledge our progress. Sharing your progress with a friend, family member, or spouse might help you internalize your accomplishments and feel more gratified. It also allows everyone around you to see how hard you've worked. Sharing your journey with others can feel extremely validating, especially when you know they understand and support you.

I spoke with Karen a few weeks ago, and she has been working hard to reduce the yelling in her household. She told her sister about her victories, and she was overjoyed for her, offering words of encouragement and praise. This external validation bolstered Karen's confidence in her capacity to effect positive change.

Take some time today to discuss your progress with someone who will congratulate you. It may be your partner, a close friend, or even your children. Celebrating your progress together may make your trip feel more concrete and motivate you to keep going.

Step 5: Celebrate yourself, no matter how small the victory.

The last stage is to celebrate oneself. It's simple to dismiss successes, especially when they don't seem significant. However, congratulating yourself—whether with a tiny treat, a quiet moment of meditation, or just telling yourself, "I'm proud of what I've done"—is critical for your mental and emotional well-being.

For example, I've made it a habit to celebrate tiny triumphs. After a particularly difficult week, I'll allow myself to take a long bath, sip my favorite cup of tea, or simply sit in peace and reflect on my accomplishments. It's my method of recognizing my efforts and accomplishments.

Today, take a time to rejoice. It might be anything as simple as taking a stroll, indulging in a tiny treat, or sitting in quiet with a sense of thankfulness for the job you've done. Celebrate the journey, for every step forward is progress.

Reflection is not only about looking back—it's about leveraging the insights you've received to keep moving ahead. Today, you've pondered on your triumphs, learned from your problems, recorded your progress, shared your accomplishments, and congratulated yourself. Each of these phases is a means of reinforcing the notion that you are developing, expanding, and becoming a stronger version of yourself.

The path is seldom linear, but it doesn't make it any less important. Small, regular efforts lead to long-lasting transformation. So, while you continue your journey, keep this observation in mind. Accept the progress you've experienced and use it as motivation to continue creating the life and family you desire.

Challenge Day 7: Reflect on Your Progress and Feel Proud.

As we approach the end of this week-long endeavor, it's time to stand back and actually reflect. Today isn't about pressing forward or checking off to-do lists; instead, it's about reflecting on your progress. Let's take a break today. Let us celebrate what you've already accomplished, the trip you've taken, and how much you've evolved.

I understand that people often overlook this crucial time. We tend to focus on our shortcomings, unfinished tasks, and future goals. But right now, I want you to tilt that lens around. Consider all you've done, no matter how large or small. Because your development is significant.

Step 1: Celebrate small victories.

When I first started working on fixing my own family relationships, I felt like I wasn't making progress. I had excellent days, but there were plenty of occasions when I felt like I was failing. On one of those days, I faced a particularly challenging evening due to my toddler's refusal to go to bed. I raised my voice, and I realized that wasn't the best strategy. Instead of allowing that moment to define me, I opted to focus on the minor victory. I apologized and spoke calmly thereafter. That was progress. Small successes accumulate over time, even if they might not feel like tremendous shifts in the moment.

Perhaps you have had similar experiences. Perhaps you've seen yourself becoming more patient with your child, or maybe you're finally able to stay calm throughout those hectic morning routines. These moments are equally as significant as the major milestones. Think about those today. No victory is too minor to celebrate.

For example, my friend Linda has two small children, and her mornings were previously chaotic. She would eventually raise her voice, which made her feel bad afterwards. But in the last several weeks, she has made a concerted effort to remain calm and adhere to a morning routine. The first few days were difficult, but she now observes that mornings are much easier. She still has problems, but the fact that she has been able to remain calm on most days is a significant victory.

Take a minute now to reflect on your own minor accomplishments. Give yourself credit for each step forward.

<u>Step 2: Recognize Your Growth, Even If It Doesn't Look Perfect.</u>

Growth rarely follows a linear path and is often messy.

When I originally started this trip, I imagined it as a smooth upward arc of continuous development. However, I quickly realized that setbacks are part of the growing process. It involves blunders, difficulties, and situations that do not go as planned.

There were moments when I felt frustrated with myself for not being flawless. But here's the truth: perfection is not the aim. This is progress. Every error has taught me something useful. That one instant of raising my voice taught me to pause and breathe before reacting again. Those moments of imperfection served as stepping stones, leading me to become a better parent and more patient person.

What has your growth path been like? Consider the times when you battled and things didn't go as planned. Do you understand what those experiences have taught you? Because they, too, are valued. Those challenging experiences may force us to grow in the most significant ways.

For example, I had a coworker who was quite critical of herself when she did not match the "perfect" parenting criteria. She would be unhappy about things she didn't accomplish, but as she reflected on her trip, she saw that the manner in which she managed her child's tantrums had greatly improved. Instead of raising her voice right away, she would quietly affirm her child's emotions and reply with compassion. It wasn't always flawless, but the progress was obvious.

Remember that progress does not imply perfection. It's about making a bit more progress every day and accepting that growth occurs in different ways and at different periods.

Step 3: Compare Your "Before" with "Now"

Think back to when you initially started this challenge. What was life like then? How did you deal with your child's difficulties, how did you manage stress, and how did you feel about your ability to remain calm? Think about where you are now. What has changed?

I recall when I initially began working on my reflexes. Mornings were stressful, and I felt like I was constantly rushing to get things done. I was frequently snapping at my children, frustrated by the never-ending duties. I now add breathing exercises, clear routines, and flexibility into my mornings. Sure, there are still periods of mayhem, but my mornings are often more tranquil. That is development.

Your "before" may have felt like a continual battle, but looking back, you'll notice that even minor improvements have made a significant impact. Your daily routine, approach to confrontation, and capacity to remain cool have all improved.

Consider the changes you've made since starting this quest. Celebrate the change.

Step 4: Do not compare yourself to others.

Comparing oneself to others is one of the most significant barriers to feeling pleased with our accomplishments. It's so tempting to admire other parents and believe they have it all together, whether it's their calm attitude, immaculate routines, or seemingly beautiful children. But I can tell you this: everyone suffers. Nobody's path is flawless, and comparing yourself to others just takes away the satisfaction of your own accomplishments.

Remind yourself that your journey is unique and shouldn't look like anyone else's. Just meet your own expectations—not others'.

For example, I've felt like I wasn't doing enough when I observed a parent at school drop-off who appeared to be so orderly, calm, and put together. However, when I paused to think, I understood that my experience was unique to myself. I'd gone a long way since I started, and that was something to be proud of, even if it didn't look like everyone else's.

You deserve to be proud of your progress. Don't allow others' journeys to outshine your own.

Step 5: Take a moment to feel proud.

Finally, today is about respecting oneself. It is not about the next challenge or development. Today is about honoring all you've done, including the effort, patience, dedication, and love you've put into this trip. You deserve to be proud.

Sarah, a mother I worked with, experienced a constant sense of exhaustion. After a particularly difficult week, she sat down with a cup of tea, took a deep breath, and thought about all the measures she had taken to enhance her parenting. She didn't have a flawless week, but she had made significant improvements. She patted herself on the back, and the pride she felt that day sustained her through the next difficult moments.

Now, take some time to reflect on your trip and feel proud of yourself. You did a fantastic job. Celebrate that.

Looking back is not only a chance to recognize your accomplishments, but it also serves as motivation to keep going. After reflecting on your progress, remember that this is just the beginning. Every move, however little, is a step forward.

Feel proud of yourself. And while you continue on this path, keep in mind that progress is a process rather than a goal. Today, you have already taken an essential step.

Conclusion.

As we near the end of this book, I'd like to remind you of something important: this journey isn't about perfection. It is not about becoming a perfect parent, having flawless children, or building a perfectly tranquil home. The truth is that life is not flawless. Families are messy, routines are unpredictable, and feelings are genuine. However, we've discussed techniques, strategies, and mentality shifts in these pages to guide you toward something far more powerful than perfection: a more peaceful, connected, and resilient family.

We've talked about a variety of topics throughout this book. We've discussed ways to quit yelling, manage your emotions, and remain grounded during difficult situations. You've learned how to strengthen your relationships with your children and create a loving, trusting, and respectful atmosphere. We've also discussed how to deal with difficult parenting situations while maintaining your energy and sense of self.

However, the central idea of this book and the entire process is growth. It's about accepting who you are as a parent today while remaining open to change and progress tomorrow. By reading these words, you have already taken the first step. And now, by taking action—whether through a new habit, a better mindset, or a change in how you interact with your children—you are already influencing the future of your family.

- Embrace the process, not just the results.

Remember that this is not about quick cures or immediate outcomes. The changes you've made in recent days and weeks will take time to completely materialize. Don't expect things to fall into place overnight. There will be times of success and moments of difficulty. Both are part of the process.

Persistence is essential for achieving long-term change. You've learned to improve your outlook, manage your emotions, and prioritize yourself. You've made your home more harmonious by applying family-friendly practices. The most essential aspect of all of this is that you've discovered that little changes over time produce large outcomes.

Remember the first challenge you faced in this book? You were uncertain about how things would turn out. However, as you progressed through each day, lesson, and adjustment in viewpoint, you began to sense a transition. That is the beauty of this process: change accumulates. Every step forward, every pause before reacting, every quiet nighttime routine you establish, all add up.

The Power of Patience and Self-Compassion

If you learn anything from this book, be patient with yourself. Parenting is difficult, and occasionally you will fall short of your objectives. That is okay. We don't expect you to have everything figured out. The most vital aspect is your dedication to development, not perfection.

You've made improvements, whether it's through better communication, self-care, or a more relaxed approach to everyday stress. These things require time, and every instant of effort counts. So, when things don't go as planned, try not to be too harsh on yourself. Treat yourself with the same care that you are learning to show your children.

For example, there have been times when I felt like starting all over again. Maybe I raised my voice or didn't reply as quietly as I wanted. But then I remind myself of my progress. I tell myself that parenthood is a marathon, not a sprint. Every day, I discover something new about myself and my children, which is a win in and of itself.

- A Stronger and More Resilient Family

Our journey is about creating a family, not just you as a parent. You and your children are learning to grow together as they go through ups and downs, tension, and peaceful periods. You are teaching children how to negotiate emotions, form positive connections, and overcome problems with resilience. These are lessons that they will carry with them throughout their lives.

By focusing on respect, trust, and open communication, you are laying the groundwork for a healthier family. When you demonstrate calmness, empathy, and emotional management, your children learn to do the same. They absorb these teachings even while you are not aware of them. Your constancy, efforts to improve, and readiness to change will influence their knowledge of how to interact with the environment.

You are enough.

This book revolves around one basic truth: you are enough. Parents need not be perfect, know everything, or meet everyone's expectations. You are doing your best, and that is more than sufficient.

Every move you've taken has contributed to a more tranquil and harmonious home. We are proud of your willingness to invest in yourself and your family. There is no better present you can give your children than a household full of love, trust, respect, and understanding. And by embracing this path, you are already making that gift every day.

Moving forward: Keep going!

As we end this book, I'd like to encourage you to keep pushing forward. We must develop the tools and tactics we've discussed as habits over time, not as one-time fixes. Continue to implement them, reflect on your progress, and be gentle with yourself when things don't go as planned.

Remember that change takes time, and the most important thing is to continue showing up.

You've got it. There will be bumps along the way, but you have everything you need to continue establishing the family you want. Continue taking one step at a time. Continue to study, grow, and nurture your relationship with your children.

Aknowledgments.

First and foremost, I wish to express my heartfelt gratitude to my family. Your love, support, and patience served as the foundation for this book. Thank you for your consistent support and understanding, even when the hours spent writing distracted me from our time together. You've taught me the importance of connection, compassion, and resilience—the very concepts that this book seeks to communicate with others.

A special thank you to my kids. You're the reason this book exists. Your passion, questions, and unique perspectives have shown me that the essence of parenting lies in periods of personal development, peaceful relationships, and mutual comprehension. I wrote this book with the intention of learning as much from you as imparting knowledge. I hope that one day you will read this and appreciate the love, care, and commitment that went into each page.

My editor's knowledge, patience, and vision have guided me throughout this trip. Your ability to see the large picture while focusing on the details contributed to the success of this book. Your careful feedback and unflinching support for this project made all the difference.

A heartfelt thank you to my mentors and coworkers for shaping my perspective of parenting and personal development. Your expertise has laid a solid foundation for my career, and I am grateful to have benefited from your insights. You've inspired me to believe that parenting is about intention, growth, and resilience, rather than perfection.

I'd also like to thank the many parents who have shared their experiences, problems, and accomplishments with me. Your feedback, whether through discussions, emails, or shared experiences, helped form the message of this book. This book is a reflection of our shared experiences, and I am grateful for your openness, courage, and willingness to share.

Dear readers, thank you for entrusting me with your time and travel. Parenting is not simple, but it is the most important labor we can do. I am honored to be a part of your parenting journey with this book, and I hope it equips you with the necessary tools, insights, and support to foster a loving, respectful, and harmonious household.

Finally, I want to thank the many voices in the parenting and psychological communities who continue to inspire me through their research, books, and articles. Your work is vital, and it reinforces my faith in the power of compassion and beneficial parenting.

RESOURCES.

https://www.ahaparenting.com

https://www.nytimes.com/2019/05/02/opinion/emotional-intelligence-kids-parenting.html.

https://hbr.org/2020/05/how-to-teach-your-kids-emotional-intelligence

https://www.parentingscience.com

https://www.nytimes.com/2019/06/28/opinion/raising-resilient-kids.html

https://www.parentingscience.com

https://www.ahaparenting.com

https://www.parenting.com

https://www.parentingscience.com

https://www.verywellfamily.com

FREE GIFT

As a way of saying thanks for your purchase, I'm offering the book Shadow Work Journal: A Journey of Self-Discovery for FREE to my readers.

To get instant access just go to:

Inside the book, you will discover:

- How to uncover hidden aspects of yourself through guided prompts

- Techniques for integrating your shadow self into your conscious life

- Exercises to foster emotional growth and self-awareness

- Practical tips for creating a balanced and fulfilling life

If you want to embark on a journey of self-discovery and transformation, make sure to grab the free book.

Dedicatória

Aos que me ensinaram a ler e a escrever.

GOTÍCULAS DA ALMA

Agradecimentos

Agradeço aos que me ensinaram a escrever e a ler.

Agradeço aos que escreveram para que eu também pudesse ler.

Agradeço aos que dedicaram parte do seu tempo para me ler.

GOTÍCULAS DA ALMA

Sumário

Apresentação 9
Dois 11
Mulher 12
Gaveta vazia 13
As panelas do cavalheiro 15
Bicicleta velha 21
Faltas 24
O egoísmo desprendido 25
Resignação 29
A religião e o ópio 33
O circo e a política 41
À beira do rio 44
Máquinas caça-níqueis 45
As "PatiFarias" 48
Bela vista 49
Linda, para as inimigas 55
A menina da tapera 57
Dia da mulher 70
Ferro velho 71
As pirâmides sociais 77
Mulher bonita 85
Lembranças eternas 86
Herança 87

Experiência.. 94

Feminismo e acumulação de riqueza 95

Simbiose perfeita 115

Residência... 121

Guerra aos pijamas 126

Aeroporto 127

Emoções 129

Ser e estar... 142

Olhares 143

Louco... 150

O som da chuva 151

As gotículas e o oceano 153

Apresentação

Os textos deste livro pretendem exprimir gotículas da realidade concreta da alma de seres humanos e do convívio entre eles.

Sempre priorizei atividades relacionadas às áreas da contabilidade e dos direitos tributário e financeiro - nesta me dedicando às operações financeiras, finanças e dívidas públicas -, mas ao completar setenta e quatro anos de vida, amparando-me no ensinamento de grandes autores que dizem que as pessoas escrevem para si mesmas, resolvi dedicar parte do meu tempo para escrever para mim.

Porém, mesmo tendo escrito estes textos para mim, fico contente só em pensar que alguém possa eventualmente dedicar parte do seu tempo para lê-los.

Assim, escrevi esses textos heterogêneos e em linguagem coloquial distensa na forma de contos (ou seriam descontos?), poesias (ou seriam heresias?), poemas (ou seriam blasfemas?) e crônicas (ou seriam nicas?) onde, entre outros, percorro ligeiramente temas sobre 1) a exaltação às mulheres, 2) o feminismo como fator de acumulação de riqueza, 3) a vida de uma catadora de materiais recicláveis, 4) o falso conceito de uma única pirâmide social, 5) o homicídio sob violenta emoção, 6) o erro da comparação da religião com o ópio e 7) o automóvel como máquina de arrecadar impostos.

Portanto, não sei ao certo o que estes textos são, mas sei que eu os sinto como gotículas da minha alma que derramo sobre essas páginas para que elas se desloquem de olho em olho, de dispositivo em dispositivo e de ouvido em ouvido e se transformem em névoa ao serem jogadas em ambiente quente, em pedras em ambiente gelado e em pensamentos em ambiente meditativo.

De qualquer modo, o importante é que, nestes ou em quaisquer outros ambientes, essas gotículas da minha alma permaneçam com os que lhes concederem refúgio, mesmo que por um brevíssimo tempo.

Dois

Um caminho,
um horizonte,
um corpo,
uma alma.

Somos só nossos!

Mulher

Pode ser cruel,
pode ser algoz,
pode ser ferina,
pode ser perversa,
pode ser ciumenta,
pode ser impiedosa,
pode ser implacável,
pode ser encrenqueira.

Mas ... porém ... todavia ... contudo ...

ela é adorável,
ela é reverenciável,
ela é imprescindível!

Gaveta vazia

Não, não coloques nada na gaveta, meu amor.
Gaveta vazia é o amor em primazia.
Nada na gaveta, por favor, meu amor.
Para o amor sobreviver, a gaveta deve permanecer
vazia.

Não gostastes de algo, fale, por favor, meu amor.
Vamos dialogar, para poder ajustar, meu amor.
Sejamos valentes para manter o nosso amor.
Sejamos sinceros para manter o nosso amor.
Sejamos empáticos para manter o nosso amor.
Sejamos competentes para manter o nosso amor.

Não, não coloques nada na gaveta, meu amor.
Gaveta vazia é o amor em primazia.
Nada na gaveta, por favor, meu amor.
Para o amor sobreviver, a gaveta deve permanecer
vazia.

O amor necessita de diálogo.
O amor necessita de valentia.
O amor necessita de sinceridade.
O amor necessita de empatia.
O amor necessita de competência.

Não, não coloques nada na gaveta, meu amor.
Gaveta vazia é o amor em primazia.
Nada na gaveta, por favor, meu amor.
Para o amor sobreviver, a gaveta deve permanecer
vazia.

Guardar desconfortos na gaveta, é covardia.
Guardar desconfortos na gaveta, é falsidade.

Guardar desconfortos na gaveta, é descaso.
Guardar desconfortos na gaveta, é incompetência.

Não, não coloques nada na gaveta, meu amor.
Gaveta vazia é o amor em primazia.
Nada na gaveta, por favor, meu amor.
Para o amor sobreviver, a gaveta deve permanecer
vazia.

Guardar desconfortos na gaveta é armazenar
munição.
Armazenar munição é preparar a briga.
Preparar a briga mostra que o amor já se foi.
Se o amor já se foi por que esperar?
Se o amor já se foi, por que brigar?
Enquanto a gaveta está vazia, o amor continua.
Enquanto a gaveta está vazia, a felicidade continua.

Não, não coloques nada na gaveta, meu amor.
Gaveta vazia é o amor em primazia.
Nada na gaveta, por favor, meu amor.
Para o amor sobreviver, a gaveta deve permanecer
vazia.

As panelas do cavalheiro

O momento era lindo.

Uma sensação de paz e de harmonia a envolvia inteiramente.

Ela estava tomada por uma felicidade impossível de descrever, pois qualquer descrição seria imperfeita.

As meninas ora corriam livres e ora se deitavam no campo e ficavam olhando o passar das pequenas e alvas nuvens iluminadas pelos raios dourados daquele sol primaveril.

Os meninos corriam montados em galhos secos que haviam caído da árvore que proporcionava a ela uma agradabilíssima sombra.

A ponta mais grossa do galho que os meninos seguravam com suas pequeninas mãos era a cabeça e o pescoço, a ponta mais fina era o rabo, os pezinhos deles eram as patas e uma das mãos traçava pequenas elipses no ar impelindo aquele imaginário garboso cavalo.

O campo onde ela estava deitada e as crianças brincavam era forrado com uma suave relva verde de onde sobressaíam pequeninas flores amarelas e azuis com cores tão vívidas que até pareciam gotículas caídas daquele ensolarado céu azul, que ela sentia como se fosse um aconchegante e protetor manto que acobertava a todos eles.

A sensação de leveza que ela sentia era sublime, divina, até.

Todo aquele ambiente formava um quadro encantador, de uma beleza ímpar.

De repente, o barulho: blam, blam, blam.

A cama sacudia vigorosamente.

O cérebro dela ficou tomado de enorme confusão entre o sonho e a realidade.

Deitado, o marido batia a perna direita no colchão.

Ela não conseguia separar as cenas.

As do sonho maravilhoso se intercalavam e se confundiam com aquele barulho ameaçador.

As imagens e os sons do campo e das crianças se misturavam velozmente com a imagem e os sons da cama e do marido.

A perna dele voltou a bater sobre o colchão e desta vez com tanta força que o sonho acabou abruptamente e a realidade se impôs com enorme intensidade.

- O que houve? - perguntou ela.

- Não vais preparar o desjejum? – respondeu ele, rispidamente.

Ela andava exausta e precisava de mais um pouco de sono para se recuperar do cansaço decorrente do intenso trabalho cotidiano.

Naquela manhã, a exaustão era tanta que o seu corpo parecia estar fortemente colado ao colchão.

Tão fortemente colado, que havia uma perfeita simbiose entre o corpo dela e aquela cama vestida com lençóis e colchas que ela mesmo havia confeccionado e delicadamente bordado com suas jovens mãos para compor o enxoval, que toda a noiva tinha que fazer para demonstrar as suas habilidades ao futuro marido.

Ela precisava de um pouco mais de repouso, mesmo o que fosse por um brevíssimo tempo.

- Estou exausta - disse ela.

- Só mais um pouquinho e já me levanto para preparar o alimento.

- Não - disse ele, mais grosseiramente ainda.

- Tu vais me atrasar para o meu encontro.

Ele gostava tanto daqueles encontros diários com os amigos, com o jogo de cartas e com a bebida que a sua casa, os seus filhos e a sua esposa sempre ficavam em segundo plano.

- Só mais um tiquinho de tempo - implorou ela.

- Eu juro, só um tiquinho.

- Não! chega de lamúrias, eu não gastei todo aquele dinheiro para montar a cozinha e comprar todas aquelas panelas para ficares dormindo.

- Chega!

- Levanta-te!

- Vai!

Naquele exato momento, ela sentiu um estalo em seu cérebro que a colocou em estado de serenidade, que lhe propiciou o sentimento de aceitação da dificuldade e a certeza de que tudo iria melhorar.

Ela se cala, se levanta, vai à cozinha e prepara um farto desjejum.

Ele se levanta, vai tomar banho e veste-se com as meias de fino algodão branco, com as preferidas cuecas de seda branca, com uma camisa branca de punhos rendados, que ela havia lavado, alvejado e passado no dia anterior, e completa o figurino com uma calça de brim beje.

Ele chega na sala das refeições, olha o alimento que ela havia recém preparado, e, ainda de pé, coloca as grandes mãos sobre o encosto da cadeira, inclina o corpo para a frente, baixa a cabeça e fica observando os alimentos requintadamente colocados sobre a mesa.

Ela o observava: ele ainda guardava os lindos traços do jovem rapaz cavalheiro, que havia lhe roubado o primeiro beijo, que, mesmo tendo sido um leve roçar de lábios, havia impregnado nela a sensação de um fervoroso e longo beijo.

Por longo tempo, cada vez que pensava naquele fugaz momento, ela ainda ficava com a pele do rosto enrubescida e a respiração ofegante.

As sensações de felicidade e de culpa a dominavam: ela permitiu? ela possibilitou? ela queria? ela provocou? ela havia pecado?

Estas perguntas passavam pelo seu cérebro como um vendaval arrasador, mas a única resposta era de que tinha sido um momento mágico e que tinha sido o passo inicial para o namoro, o noivado e o casamento deles.

Ele ergue a cabeça em direção a ela e, com ares de superioridade típico dos narcisistas, pergunta:

- É isso que tens para me oferecer?

Ele endireita o corpo, tira as mãos da cadeira e vocifera:

- Vou comer no restaurante!

Vai até a porta de saída da casa, veste o casaco da mesma cor beje das calças, que ela havia escovado no dia anterior, coloca um lenço vermelho em volta do pescoço e sai batendo a porta sem se despedir, nem dela nem das crianças.

Ele vinha tendo este tipo de comportamento há muitos anos e a cada dia que passava ficava mais intenso e mais rude.

Ela analisa todo aquele momento e fica com uma dúvida: - o seu lindo cavalheiro havia se transformado no cavalo e na panela dos amigos, da bebida e do jogo?

Mas ela continuava cada vez mais serena e pensava: - as dificuldades vão passar e tudo vai melhorar.

Ela tira a mesa, lava os pratos, os talheres, as panelas, deixa-os reluzentes e guarda-os perfeitamente alinhados como quando eles foram comprados para estruturar o que viria a ser o idealizado lar da família.

Enquanto arruma os filhos com as roupas que usavam no dia a dia, ela lembra de cada uma das quatro gestações desde os exames pré-natais, as idas ao hospital para os partos e as voltas para casa com os bebês quando, por morar longe de parentes, sempre estava somente acompanhada de uma ou de outra amiga.

Cantarolando uma bela música infantil abre a porta da casa, acolhe as crianças com seus braços e mãos, dá uma olhada para trás e uma lágrima rola em sua face.

Ela sabia que não conseguiria mais voltar para aquela casa nem que fosse somente para buscar as roupas das crianças.

Sabia também que enfrentaria sérias dificuldades, principalmente, financeiras.

Mas, mesmo assim, ela fecha suavemente a porta, passa a chave, que havia utilizado por vários anos, por baixo da porta e empurra-a para dentro da casa.

E, com seus filhos ... serenamente ... foi!

Sem mágoas, sem ressentimentos, sem frustrações ... simplesmente ... foi!

E foi para nunca mais voltar!

Bicicleta velha

Amanhece.

É feriado.

Em silêncio, ela se levantou.

O levantar dela, o prostrou.

Ao amanhecer, a vida dele anoitecia!

Eram seis horas da manhã e a previsão do tempo indicava que o dia seria ensolarado e teria uma temperatura amena, condições que convidavam para um prazeroso passeio a dois.

Após ter se levantado da cama, a sua amada tirou o pijama e colocou uma blusa e uma bermuda que, coladas ao seu corpo, delinearam perfeitamente todas as suas belas curvas.

Ela desceu para a garagem, retirou a bicicleta do gancho que a suspendia do chão, verificou a pressão dos pneus, examinou todo o conjunto e colocou os óculos, as luvas e o capacete multicolorido com tons onde predominava o amarelo alaranjado, típico das chamas ardentes.

Suavemente, caminhou até a saída, passou a perna sobre o quadro, posicionou o pé no pedal, impulsionou a bicicleta e se sentou sobre o selim sem se importar com o desconforto que a rigidez dele lhe causava.

Ela foi andar de bicicleta, foi pedalar, com as amigas.

Ele se sentiu como uma bicicleta velha e imprestável: sem rodas, sem pedais, sem selim, com o quadro enferrujado e com meio guidom.

Essa troca deixou-o consciente que, naquele alvorecer, o seu anoitecer havia chegado.

Sentiu-se destroçado, pois pressentia que nunca mais sentiria o pedalar, o rebolar, o suor, o esforço, a dedicação e o farfalhar da blusa dela, que o deixaram feliz por tanto tempo.

- O tempo, ah, esse implacável tempo - falou em voz alta para se ouvir e se resignar.

Pensou, remoeu os pensamentos, concluiu que o seu prazo havia vencido e resolveu desaparecer.

Em sua mente o rumo dele estava claro: o caminhão da sucata.

Quando ele estava sentindo ser conduzido para o alto forno siderúrgico, onde veria acabar aquela sua existência, um alento lhe sobreveio.

Desde o primeiro instante da entrada no local do forno até o momento do seu consumo final ele voltaria a sentir o calor e os efeitos das labaredas que o consumiram durante os gloriosos dias que tinha vivido com ela.

- Bons e velhos tempos que rapidamente desapareciam - falou em voz alta.

Ela voltou para casa, recolocou a bicicleta no gancho, tirou os óculos, as luvas e o capacete e se dirigiu para o desejado banho.

Colocou o pijama, andou pelas dependências da casa e sentiu-a fria, silenciosa e vazia.

Sentou-se na poltrona que havia no quarto e lembrou do passeio e das risadas e sentiu uma agradável ardência nos músculos das panturrilhas e nas coxas e uma gostosa dor no assoalho pélvico provocada pela rigidez do selim fino e pequeno.

Olhou o relógio e verificou que desde o levantar até aquele momento haviam decorrido seis horas.

Levantou-se da poltrona e deitou-se na grande cama vazia e pensou nas dezoito horas que ainda faltavam para completar aquele dia e passou a se perguntar se as seis horas de pedalada preencheriam as próximas dezoito horas, que também se anunciavam frias, silenciosas e vazias.

Pensando que pudesse ser o sentimento de solidão se instalando em seu ser, uma forte angústia lhe dominou.

Algumas perguntas surgiram e permaneceram rodando na mente dela:

- Foram momentos alegres, mas estou feliz? é isso que eu quero para minha vida? está valendo?

Enquanto isso, ele, que tinha virado uma nuvem de fumaça, vagueava à procura de uma alma amorosa que o materializasse novamente.

Faltas

Eu não sinto a falta do teu pé para substituir as meias para dormir.

Eu não sinto a falta do teu corpo para substituir o cobertor da cama.

Eu sinto a falta ...
do teu corpo,
do teu andar,
do teu abraço,
do teu sorriso,
do teu carinho.

Eu sinto a falta ...
da tua mão,
da tua boca,
da tua coxa,
da tua perna,
da tua atenção,
da tua conversa,
da tua presença.

A tua falta provoca em mim a falta da minha energia vital.

Sem ti, eu não existo!

O egoísmo desprendido

Eles resolveram passar um período sabático para conversar sobre a relação deles.

Combinaram que não seria um daqueles momentos do conhecido "dr", o "discutir a relação", que normalmente ocorrem quando os ânimos já estão alterados, mas um momento em que se comprometiam a ficar serenos, sem agitação e sem estremecimentos.

Em boa parte do tempo, eles viviam alegres, mas queriam mais, queriam ser felizes.

A alegria sempre foi fácil de ser alcançada, mas ela vinha e se esgotava rapidamente.

Eles almejavam a felicidade perene, mas esse era um objetivo que não estavam conseguindo alcançar.

O egoísmo, que aflorava no comportamento deles com bastante frequência por estar fortemente inserido em suas personalidades pelo modo individualista de proceder arraigado no meio social em que viviam, tanto atrapalhava o atingimento da perene felicidade que eles seguidamente se perguntavam: seria a felicidade apenas uma idealização inatingível?

Em algumas vezes, eles tinham conseguido conquistar a desejada felicidade, mas, como toda conquista requer árduo trabalho para ser mantida, ela chegava e desaparecia velozmente.

Para poderem se afastar das atividades cotidianas durante esse período, eles ajustaram os compromissos e reservaram um apartamento em hotel localizado em uma montanha onde eram praticados esportes de inverno, mas tiveram o cuidado de fazer essa reserva na estação do verão quando esses hotéis ficam praticamente vazios.

Na data acertada, eles chegaram e se acomodaram no hotel, que tinha como horizonte somente a natureza típica de regiões montanhosas e que ficava afastado do centro urbano e do burburinho de pessoas.

Nos dias que se seguiram à chegada, eles se levantavam, faziam o desjejum e saiam para caminhar e, serenamente, analisavam e debatiam o convívio cotidiano deles.

Ao passar dos dias eles foram chegando a algumas conclusões.

Uma dessas conclusões foi a de que a relação deles não podia ser como um clube onde as pessoas se reúnem para realizar atividades que são escolhidas pelo voto dos participantes ou, então, para participar de jogos onde sempre há aqueles que se consideram ganhadores e os que se consideram perdedores.

Outra conclusão foi a de que a felicidade não podia depender de uma conquista - que traz a ideia do domínio, da posse, da submissão, da captura - mas, sim, depender de um convencimento mútuo, da persuasão mútua, que são pilares absolutamente necessários para a construção de uma ampla base de sustentação de uma felicidade perene.

Também concluíram que a felicidade dependia da doação mútua, ou seja, um deveria se doar ao outro.

Mas essa doação devia ser desinteressada, portanto ela não podia ter o caráter de obrigação, pois toda obrigação traz em si uma sensação de penosidade, e muito menos podia ter o caráter de um direito, posto que inexistente.

Mas duas perguntas ainda pairavam no ar e eles necessitavam de respostas claras para elas: como fazer para anular o egoísmo que lhes impregnava? quais seriam as atitudes que deveriam adotar para que ambos atingissem essa necessária persuasão, esse necessário convencimento mútuo, essa doação desinteressada?

Nos últimos dias do período que haviam reservado, conseguiram chegar às respostas, que eles sabiam ser indispensáveis.

Concordaram que uma das atitudes centrais que precisavam ter era a de que eles precisavam aceitar as ideias um do outro, ou seja, era necessário introjetar a verdade de que ninguém é o dono da razão e tão pouco tem ideias imutáveis, pois, afinal, qualquer um, em até pequenos lapsos de tempo, pode ter opiniões que confrontadas se mostram antagônicas entre si.

Outra concordância a que chegaram era a de que o relacionamento deles não podia ser um contrato transitório durante o qual um ou os dois procuram apenas destacar os seus individualismos.

Diante dessas duas concordâncias, colocaram-se a pensar e chegaram à conclusão de que um seria feliz se, e somente se, o outro também fosse feliz, ou seja, a felicidade de um dependia da felicidade do outro.

Portanto, concluíram que ambos agindo egoisticamente, com o egoísmo que lhes impregnava e do qual não conseguiam se livrar, atingiriam a felicidade mútua e perene quando internalizassem o seguinte princípio de conduta: EU vou te fazer feliz para EU ser feliz.

À noite, deitados, eles se sentiam como se fossem um só corpo e de mãos dadas, deitados, pelados, suados e colados um ao outro experimentando o calor e uma maravilhosa energia que emanavam dos seus corpos e mentes, passaram a projetar o caminho que construiriam para percorrer juntos.

Resignação

Ela pega e telefone e liga para um número que lembra de memória.

- Oi, mãe, tudo bem? – atende o filho.

Ela responde e faz um pedido.

- Sim, está tudo bem, filho.

- Podes vir aqui em casa para conversarmos?

- Claro que sim, em seguida chego aí.

- Muito obrigado, - respondeu ela.

O filho chega, levemente preocupado, mas contente por ter ido falar com aquela mulher que ele ama com toda a intensidade do seu ser.

- Oi, mãe, como estás bem, estás alegre, disposta e me pareces contente.

- Sim, filho, graças a Deus, estou me sentido muito bem.
Ambos se sentam nas cadeiras que estão colocadas em frente ao fogão a lenha, que está fornecendo um calor agradável e aconchegante.

Ela tinha acendido o fogão, colocado sobre a chapa uma chaleira de ferro com água e preparado a cuia do chimarrão.

Em silêncio, ela encheu a cuia e tomou o primeiro mate para deixar a erva bem compactada e sem aquele gosto forte provocado por um pouco do pó da erva que sobe pela bomba junto com a água.

Ainda em silêncio, ela encheu a cuia novamente e a passou para o seu filho com a erva já no seu ponto correto.

Também em silêncio, ele sorveu todo o líquido até ouvir o roncar da bomba, que é a indicação de que toda a água servida na cuia foi devidamente consumida, um dos ensinamentos que havia aprendido na casa paterna.

Lá pela quarta rodada, ela falou.

- Tu sabes que estou com muitas saudades do teu pai.

- Já se vão dois anos da morte dele, mas a cada dia que passa eu sinto um aperto cada vez maior no meu coração, pois ele me faz muita falta.

- Não sei se percebestes, mas na última vez que me levastes no cemitério para visitar o tumulo dele eu não consegui conter as lágrimas.

- Sim, eu percebi, mãe, e lembro que eu também fiquei comovido, pois eu também sinto muita falta do meu querido velho.

- As tuas lágrimas me deixaram muito feliz porque eu percebi o quanto tu o amavas.

- Mas as tuas lágrimas me deixaram também muito surpreso porque naquele momento eu descobri que eu nunca havia te visto chorar.

- Ao te ver chorar senti o quanto tu és forte, porque vocês dois passaram muitas dificuldades e mesmo assim vocês nunca choraram na nossa frente.

- Que o pai não chorasse até fazia sentido porque ele foi criado em uma época em que o homem não podia chorar, mas tu, como mulher, podias chorar e mesmo assim nunca te permitistes que os teus filhos te visem abatida.

- Muito obrigado, mãe.

Ambos ficaram em silêncio por mais uma rodada do chimarrão e ela voltou a falar.

- Bem, meu filho, mas não era sobre isso que eu queria falar contigo.

- Eu queria te pedir que na próxima vez que eu estiver com algum problema de saúde tu não me leves mais para o hospital.

- Como assim, mãe?

- Me explica melhor esse teu pedido, pois eu terei muita dificuldade para atendê-lo.

- Acontece que na última vez que fui hospitalizada eles fizerem alguns exames que me deixaram muito desconfortável e eu não quero que isso aconteça novamente.

- Mas, mãe, é meu dever cuidar da tua saúde e da tua vida.

- Como eu posso atender esse teu pedido, como posso deixar de te cuidar?

- Tu, disse ela com forte voz de comando, cuida da tua família até que eles andem com as próprias pernas e não precisem mais de teus cuidados diários.

- Como vocês, meus filhos, não precisam mais de mim, eu estou pronta para partir para a vida eterna, na qual sempre acreditei, pois eu fiz a minha parte!

Como a mensagem havia sido dada e compreendida, eles continuaram, em silêncio, tomando chimarrão.

Quando a erva já havia ficado sovada, eles se despediram com um longuíssimo e apertado abraço.

A religião e o ópio

Os dois se encontraram na mesma mesa do bar onde sempre se reuniam no final da tarde para tomar um café, uma água e conversar sobre o dia a dia deles e da sociedade em que viviam.

- Hoje voltei a ouvir a expressão de que "a religião é o ópio do povo" – disse o mais velho.

- Sim, - disse o mais jovem – é uma expressão bastante citada quando são debatidas as obras de vários filósofos sobre religiões.

- Pois é, disse o mais velho, mas eu fiquei pensando se essa expressão ainda se aplica nos nossos tempos.

- A propósito, lembro de um texto que li há muitos anos onde o autor, do qual infelizmente não lembro o nome, afirmava que diante do enorme consumo de drogas, tanto as ditas lícitas quanto as ditas ilícitas, que se verificava em nossa sociedade, talvez fosse o caso de inverter a ordem das palavras passando-se a afirmar que "o ópio é a religião do povo".

O mais jovem ficou pensando alguns minutos e ponderou:

- Mas alguns filósofos afirmavam que as religiões eram utilizadas para alienar as populações das realidades sociais.

E continuou o mais jovem.

- Aliás, essa expressão chegou a ser adaptada ao futebol quando algumas pessoas afirmavam que "o futebol é o ópio do povo".

- Bem, meu caro jovem, mas creio que aí essas pessoas exageraram na dose, afinal, o futebol é um dos lazeres das pessoas e, sem sombra de dúvidas, o lazer é essencial para a vida saudável do ser humano.

Voltando ao assunto inicial, o mais velho continuou.

- Creio que também estavam exagerando aqueles filósofos que tentaram desqualificar as religiões ao compará-las com aquele narcótico.

- Pelo que lemos na história humana, os povos sempre tiveram as suas religiões e quando uma ou outra deixasse de ser praticada ou fosse desqualificada outra era fundada para ocupar o espaço vazio, e isso ocorre ainda hoje o que demonstra que os seres humanos não conseguem viver sem uma religião, uma seita, uma crença ou uma fé que os conectem com o divino, com o transcendental, com o sobrenatural.

E continuou o mais velho.

- A vinculação do homem ao divino está presente inclusive naquelas sociedades que seguem ao pé da letra partes de escrituras que reportam sobre divindades rancorosas, vingadoras e belicosas.

- Assim, creio ser possível afirmar que todo o ser humano está indelevelmente vinculado a uma divindade, mesmo sendo ela um produto da imaginação.

- Além de serem utilizadas para a conexão com o divino, as religiões preenchem a necessidade das pessoas de terem o sentimento de pertencimento ao oferecerem o aconchego daquele grupo social que as praticam e, com isso, elas evitam que as pessoas busquem esse mesmo aconchego em grupos de pessoas que se organizam para praticar atos que são nocivos à sociedade por se sentirem ilhadas, sozinhas, abandonadas, desamparadas, isoladas.

- Portanto, me parece que a expressão que faz analogia da religião com o ópio está extremamente equivocada.

O mais velho parou por uns instantes, pensou e continuou.

- Me parece, inclusive, que o equívoco desses filósofos deve ser reconhecido até por aqueles que se dizem deístas, racionalistas, ateístas, descrentes, materialistas ...

- Opa, me parece que essa conclusão não consegues sustentar.

- Creio que posso sustentá-la, sim, meu jovem.

- Vamos desenvolver um raciocínio sobre a importância das religiões na organização das sociedades sob um enfoque bem pragmático e realístico.

Enquanto o mais velho pensava em como iria introduzir o assunto, o mais jovem disse:

- Agora, meu velho, fiquei mais curioso ainda, pois, quando dizes que até um ateísta deveria defender uma ou outra religião, me parece que entrastes em um terreno escarpado.

Adotando uma postura professoral, o mais velho começou a explanar o seu ponto de vista.

- Veja, meu caro jovem, nos estudos que abrangeram escrituras sagradas de civilizações que existiram há várias dezenas de séculos até as dos dias de hoje os pesquisadores afirmam que a pregação da empatia e da compaixão é um ponto de convergência entre elas.

- Cada religião tem seus textos sagrados, seus guias morais, que são escritos com palavras próprias, mas, na essência, alguns preceitos imperiosos são iguais em todas elas como, por exemplo, o de não matar, não adulterar, não furtar, não dar falso testemunho e o de não cobiçar as coisas alheias.

E continuou o mais velho.

- São regras simples e claras, que todos nós concordamos que devem ser adotadas por toda e qualquer sociedade humana.

- Essas religiões também têm em comum uma outra regra que foca a saúde mental e o bem-estar das pessoas e, consequentemente, da sociedade, que é o mandamento de não trabalhar em algum dia da semana bem como nos dias do ano que são chamados de feriados.

Neste momento, o mais jovem interrompe a explanação e afirma.

- Ei, meu velho, calma lá, mas essas regras também são estabelecidas pelo Estado, ou seja, nada há de novo nisso.

- Aí é que te enganas, meu jovem, não podes te esquecer que essas regras são anteriores a qualquer lei, portanto as nossas atuais leis foram inspiradas nesses mandamentos.

O mais jovem o interrompe mais uma vez e fala.

- Tudo bem, vou concordar que as religiões tiveram um papel importante na organização das diferentes sociedades, mas, como essas regras religiosas já estão incorporadas ao arcabouço jurídico do Estado, atualmente não precisamos mais delas.

- Negativo, não podes te esquecer que as leis do Estado são continuamente alteradas, tanto para melhor quanto para pior, enquanto as regras das religiões vêm se mantendo ao longo de milênios e continuam servindo de farol tanto para a organização quanto para a reorganização das sociedades eventualmente desestruturadas.

- Está bem, mas não sejamos pessimistas e vamos considerar que, como o Estado já incorporou essas regras religiosas, dificilmente as pessoas aceitarão retrocessos nesses pontos.

- Afinal, meu velho, o Estado é formado pelas mesmas pessoas e se o Estado cumpre o seu papel as religiões se tornam totalmente desnecessárias.

Neste momento, o mais velho o interrompe.

- Ótima colocação, meu jovem, pois ela me permite te mostrar o quanto estás equivocado ao não ver a enorme diferença que existe entre o Estado e a religião na aplicação dessas regras.

- Continuando a abordar o tema somente sob o aspecto bem pragmático, bem realista, posso te assegurar que as religiões são mais importantes e muito mais eficazes que o Estado na aplicação dessas regras.

- Ei, calma lá, meu velho, as religiões não têm o poder de polícia que tem o Estado, portanto, a eficácia do Estado é, seguramente, bem mais contundente e mais efetiva que a das religiões.

- Este é um dos pontos fulcrais da questão, pois, meu caríssimo jovem, o Estado tem o poder de polícia, mas esse poder depende da existência de um pormenorizado regramento legal, seja constitucional ou infraconstitucional.

- Se uma pessoa transgride uma regra social, como, por exemplo, a de não furtar, ela só poderá ser condenada pelo Estado se houver previsão legal, se houver provas da transgressão e se houver um minucioso processo administrativo onde tudo isso fique perfeitamente comprovado.

- No entanto, se a pessoa tem interiorizada a regra religiosa ela fica muito mais inibida de transgredir o mandamento religioso de não furtar, pois ela terá receio da condenação moral do grupo social ao qual pertence assim como terá medo da condenação divina.

- Lembras, meu jovem, que as religiões ensinam para os seus seguidores que a divindade é onipresente e onisciente, ou seja, a divindade está em todos os lugares ao mesmo tempo, consegue ver tudo e está sempre presente em todos os momentos das nossas vidas.

- Portanto, enquanto o Estado age inibindo a transgressão com a possibilidade da aplicação de algum tipo de sanção como a prisão, a pecuniária ou a restritiva de direito, as religiões agem no sentido de inibir a transgressão pela consciência, pelo sistema de valores morais, da pessoa.

- Assim, a pessoa transgressora sabe que a punição do Estado só acontecerá se a transgressão vir a ser descoberta e se for legalmente provada em um detalhado processo burocrático, o que, convenhamos, pode ser fácil numa população pequena, mas é muito difícil em localidades onde habitam centenas de milhares ou de até milhões de pessoas.

- No entanto, a punição da religião não dependerá de descoberta e de comprovação, pois a divindade que aplicará a pena é testemunha da transgressão, já que ela, a divindade, está sempre, dia e noite, junto à pessoa.

- Por isso, meu jovem, fica muito claro que as religiões são muito mais eficazes que o Estado na construção de uma sociedade mais solidária, mais justa e mais harmonizada, pois elas passam a ser uma filosofia de vida que impulsiona as pessoas a terem um novo propósito.

- Assim, meu caríssimo jovem, as religiões ao transmitirem às pessoas um forte sentimento de pertencimento e uma revigorante visibilidade social lhes dá a segurança necessária para aceitarem os reveses da vida por acreditarem que nunca ficarão desamparadas.

- Além disso, a principal sensação que a religião proporciona às pessoas é a da proteção da divindade que tudo pode e que as proverão sempre que elas necessitarem.

- Assim as pessoas fortalecem profundamente as suas autoestimas, que é um sentimento fundamental para todo o ser humano.

- Pois é, meu velho, mas temos visto que pessoas se utilizam de religiões para explorar as pessoas.

- Sim, é verdade, meu jovem, e esse fato nos leva a duas constatações:

- A primeira é a de que as pessoas tanto necessitam dessa conexão com o divino que chegam ao cúmulo de permitir que pessoas inescrupulosas as manipulem.

- E a segunda constatação, é a de que as autoridades constituídas estão sendo, perigosamente, coniventes com essas pessoas manipuladoras, pois permitem que elas explorem a boa-fé e a confiança das pessoas.

- Pois é, meu velho, preciso pensar melhor sobre isso.

Como sempre, eles se despediram com um "até a próxima" e saíram.

O circo e a política

Ela chega contente e curiosa e entra na fila da bilheteria para comprar o bilhete de ingresso.

Feita a compra, entra no complexo circense e passa a observar todo o ambiente, que é formado por um pátio de chão batido onde está erguida a lona - que protege o picadeiro, as cadeiras e as arquibancadas - e onde estão estacionados alguns pequenos e velhos reboques e um velho caminhão que serve para o transporte das peças e equipamentos do circo.

Um homem serve a pipoca e responde que não sabe até quando o circo ficará naquele local, pois depende do volume de público pagante que for aparecendo dia após dia.

Iniciada a sessão, ele reaparece apresentando as atrações, empurrando equipamentos, segurando a corda dos trapezistas, abrindo e fechando a cortina e supervisionando todos os acontecimentos.

A vendedora de algodão doce reaparece como acróbata e contorcionista.

O vendedor de refrigerantes reaparece consertando a arquibancada, apresentando-se como palhaço e dirigindo uma das três motos que circulam veloz e harmonicamente dentro da esfera de aço na atração conhecida como o globo da morte.

No aparelho do trapézio voador dois sobem até as plataformas fixas.

Em um lado, o aparador - trapezista forte que se pendura de cabeça para baixo na barra pendular – balança o seu corpo em um movimento de vai e vem.

No outro lado, o volante – trapezista leve e ágil que realiza os voos livres - balançando-se na sua barra toma altura e velocidade.

Ao atingir a velocidade e o ângulo praticados em longos anos de treinamento, o volante, largando a barra pendular, lança-se ao ar, dá três saltos mortais e, ao descer, encontra as mãos do aparador que o segura firmemente.

No retorno, o volante solta-se das mãos do aparador e gira sobre si mesmo no ar e vai ao encontro da sua barra, que lhe é lançada no tempo certo pela colega que lhe dá assistência.

Quando se apresentam ao público no fim da sessão, toda a equipe transpira sincronia, companheirismo, cumplicidade e confiança.

Neste trabalho não há espaço para o individualismo, o egocentrismo, a falta de atenção e a falta de solidariedade.

Todos eles sabem muito bem o quanto é doloroso quando o público fica em silêncio, pois isto significa descontentamento e a ausência de futuro público pagante.

Ela sai do circo e põem-se a meditar sobre a relação comumente feita entre a política e o circo e conclui que o mundo do circo nada tem a ver com o mundo da má política onde vemos sobrepor-se o individualismo ao coletivo e o egocentrismo à solidariedade.

- Somos injustos e desrespeitosos quando afirmamos que os que praticam a má política estão fazendo um espetáculo circense.

- Quem dera a política fosse um circo onde os atores buscam, à exaustão, a preparação perfeita para prestar um excelente serviço aos pagantes fazendo com que estes lancem suas mãos à frente para brindá-los com ruidosos aplausos, mesmo quando algum movimento saiu errado e o ator humildemente o recomeçou.

- Definitivamente, no mundo da política, precisamos de mais circo onde tudo depende da aclamada aprovação do distinto público - concluiu a contente espectadora.

À beira do rio

Sentado sobre a pedra,
a sorte me sorrio.

Via a água passar,
enquanto esperava,
a minha sereia chegar.

Ela chegou,
alegre e tranquila,
disposta a conversar.

Os dias se passaram,
e ela se dispôs,
para meu delírio,
a namorar.

Máquinas caça-níqueis

Os dois se encontraram na mesma mesa do bar onde sempre se reuniam no final da tarde para tomar um café, uma água e conversar sobre o dia a dia deles e da sociedade em que viviam.

Do último andar do edifício, que tem todas as paredes externas envidraçadas, eles tinham uma visão panorâmica de todo o bairro e podiam observar o vai e vem dos automóveis, que naquela hora do dia lotavam todas as ruas, as avenidas e os parques de estacionamento e pareciam uma massa uniforme que escorria lentamente por todos os espaços possíveis.

- Que te parece esse movimento de carros? - Indagou o mais jovem.

- Após uma breve meditação, o mais velho respondeu.

- Pois eu não vejo automóveis, mas uma grande massa formada por pequenas máquinas caça-níqueis.

- Ei, estás delirando? - Perguntou o mais jovem.

- Não, meu caro, estou lúcido.

- Veja, para alguns doutores em ilusionismo, os ruídos que saem dos escapamentos dos automóveis têm o som de moedas caindo dentro de um cofre e para que isso tenha um fluxo contínuo eles incentivam as aquisições de automóveis que inundam as ruas e se transformam em verdadeiras máquinas caça-níqueis-móveis, pois, além dos vários tributos incidentes na compra do carro novo, eles continuarão a gerar outros tributos durante toda a vida útil, já que são vorazes consumidores de produtos e serviços fortemente tributados.

- Esta sanha arrecadatória é alavancada pela transferência da frota antiga, que é a que mais gasta com produtos e serviços tributáveis, para pessoas de menor renda que, ao adquirirem um automóvel pensam que estão melhorando a sua condição de vida.

- Aliás, os governantes para aumentarem a quantidade destes caça-níqueis-móveis, permitem maldades como o do financiamento de longuíssimo prazo, com a cobrança de altas taxas de juros reais, sem se preocuparem com o endividamento das famílias e muito menos com o alto custo de operação e de manutenção desse bem de consumo durável.

- Aliás, muitas famílias contratam operações de leasing para adquirirem um automóvel sem ter a mínima ideia de que operação é essa e, pior, acreditam que estão comprando um patrimônio quando, na realidade, estão fazendo uma sofisticada operação financeira de aluguel do automóvel com opção de compra no final do contrato.

Refletindo sobre a exposição da ideia, o mais jovem afirma:

- É, o que afirmas faz bastante sentido, mas o automóvel é um sonho para muitos de nós.

- Eu mesmo quando comprei o meu primeiro carro me senti mais independente e isso elevou consideravelmente a minha autoestima.

- Sim, tens razão - disse o mais velho.

- E é justamente aí, nesse ponto, que o incentivo para a compra do automóvel mostra a sua maior crueldade.

- Como assim, me explica melhor isso.

- Em primeiro lugar, essa política explora esse sonho que todos temos de possuir um automóvel, em segundo lugar, ela cria uma falsa sensação de prosperidade pessoal e, em terceiro lugar, ela é economicamente contraproducente, pois só contribui para uma maior concentração de renda nas mãos da cadeia produtiva da indústria automobilística e dos rentistas que financiam as operações.

- Sim, me parece que tens razão, vou pensar nisso, meu caro decano.

- Despedindo-se com um "até a próxima", ambos saíram.

As "PatiFarias"

Elas circulam em ambientes públicos e privados, livres, leves, saltitantes, provocadoras e irritantes em um caminhar socialmente devastador e rendendo contínuas homenagens aos seus criadores: os patifes!

Bela vista

Uma vez por semana, ela passava naquela rodovia indo para o trabalho e depois voltando para casa.

Duas placas instaladas em ambos os lados da rodovia lhe chamavam a atenção, pois sempre estavam bem visíveis e extremamente limpas.

Elas tinham como cor de fundo um azul celeste e sobre ele estavam retratadas pequenas e alvíssimas nuvens.

Na parte de cima das placas estava escrito *"Canto do Repouso"* e logo abaixo *"cama, comida, bebida e bela vista"*.

Apesar de poder olhar as placas por brevíssimos momentos, pois ela sempre dirigia em alta velocidade, aquelas placas lhe transmitiam uma indescritível sensação de paz e de aconchego o que lhe fazia ficar pensativa.

- Que estranho, falou ela para si mesma em alto e bom som, como pode uma mera placa me fazer ficar tão tranquila?

- Puxa, que coisa, continuava ela a falar para si mesma, nem os remédios que a médica me receitou e que eu tomo religiosamente todos os dias antes de deitar me transmitem essa sensação tão boa.

A uns duzentos metros após aquelas placas aparecia, em um lugar ermo e no lado norte da rodovia, um acesso a um estreito caminho onde havia uma placa idêntica às outras, porém em um tamanho bem menor e com o acréscimo de uma seta que indicava que aquela era a entrada para o "*Canto do Repouso*".

O caminho mais parecia uma trilha, pois era estreito, de chão batido, onde mal passaria um automóvel por vez e era cercado de um mato bem fechado, que não permitia que a partir da rodovia fosse visualizado o que podia ser encontrado após nele entrar.

A cada vez que ela passava por lá a curiosidade aumentava e todas as vezes ela se perguntava:

- O que deve ser esse "*Canto do Repouso*"?

E continuou falando para si mesma, que era uma forma de ela se sentir menos sozinha durante o tempo que dirigia.

- Puxa, que coisa, esse local me parece ser tão enigmático, tão belo, tão atrativo, tão sedutor e, ao mesmo tempo, me parece ser tão perigoso, no entanto ele me desperta tanto atenção que até me parece ser um "canto da sereia" de que tanto fala a literatura e a mitologia.

Ela pensava no real sentido desta metáfora, que significa uma tentação, uma sedução, que pode levar as pessoas a se colocarem em situações perigosas.

Um dia, dirigindo no sentido norte da rodovia, olhou aquela placa, reduziu a velocidade, pensou várias vezes, e decidiu entrar naquele caminho que lhe causava tanta curiosidade e atração.

A medida que avançava com seu automóvel por aquele caminho, o ritmo da batida do seu coração aumentava, a boca foi ficando seca, os pés passaram a tremer e uma profunda angústia foi tomando conta de todo o seu ser e gerando uma enorme inquietação e uma forte tensão muscular.

Toda aquela situação a deixou tão preocupada que já estava com dificuldade de concentração e isso lhe transmitiu uma tão forte sensação de perigo que, após a terceira curva, decidiu frear o automóvel e falou consigo mesma:

- Acho que não devo seguir adiante, pois essa sensação de perigo está muito forte e, assim, creio que devo seguir aquela orientação que seguidamente leio nas placas que orientam o trânsito nas rodovias: "NA DÚVIDA, NÃO ULTRAPASSE".

- Sim, é isso, vou voltar, falou, decididamente, para ela mesma.

- Mas como vou voltar se esse caminho não tem espaço para manobrar o carro e eu não gosto de dirigir de ré? – ela falou mais alto para se ouvir bem.

- E se quando eu estiver voltando de ré algum outro automóvel chegar atrás de mim, o que vou fazer?

- E como vou fazer essas curvas de ré se andando para a frente já foi difícil fazê-las de tão apertadas que são?

De repente, ela parou de pensar nas coisas que talvez não dessem certo, respirou profundamente por três vezes e decidiu voltar de ré com muito cuidado, já que a apreensão e até o medo de seguir em frente era muito maior do que o medo de enfrentar as dificuldades de dirigir de ré.

Após muitos arranhões na lataria provocadas pela vegetação que a raspavam quando ela, até por estar ofegante, ansiosa e com o suor correndo pela fronte e pelas mãos, errava na condução do automóvel, ela conseguiu voltar à rodovia.

Parou o automóvel no acostamento, sentiu o alívio de ter saído daquela situação e pôs-se a dirigir para o seu destino.

Nos meses seguintes, ela continuou a rotina de passar semanalmente por aquela rodovia e as placas continuavam lá, cuidadosamente visíveis e limpas.

À medida que o tempo passava, ela foi minimizando o medo e a apreensão que havia sentido naquela tentativa que havia feito de conhecer o tal *Canto do Repouso*" e a curiosidade sobre o local voltou a fazer parte do seu cotidiano, pois além de pensar quando das passagens semanais ela também passou a pensar naquele local todos os dias e durante todas as noites quando perdia o sono.

Aquela situação estava lhe causando tanto incômodo mental, que numa determinada manhã ela decidiu:

- Na próxima semana eu vou entrar naquele caminho e vou até o fim e vou pôr um ponto final nisso e, de uma vez por todas, irei verificar o que vem a ser esse tal *"Canto do Repouso"*.

- Afinal, continuou ela a falar para si mesma, eu voltei a sentir aquela sensação de paz e de aconchego todas as vezes em que passo por lá e, se esse local me deixa pensando nele de uma forma tão intensa, ele não deve me trazer nem risco físico nem risco reputacional.

Assim como havia decidido, na semana seguinte ela entrou na rodovia tendo como primeiro destino o tal *"Canto do Repouso"*.

Chegando ao local do acesso, ela, decidida, entrou e rapidamente venceu a distância que separava a rodovia do local onde ficava o tal *"Canto do Repouso"*.

No final do caminho, ela viu uma pequena e simples casa que tinha as mesmas cores das placas - a cor de fundo um azul celeste e sobre ele pequenas e alvíssimas nuvens - e pendurada no alpendre da única porta da casa havia uma placa com os mesmos dizeres: *"Canto do Repouso"* e logo abaixo *"cama, comida, bebida e bela vista"*.

Ela estacionou no pequeno pátio, aguardou uns minutos, desceu do automóvel, olhou detidamente todo o local e não enxergou nada que pudesse vir a ser considerado como uma bela vista.

Começou a caminhar lentamente em direção àquela pequena casa quando, de repente, a porta foi suavemente aberta e apareceu sobre os degraus uma mulher de meia idade, com uma bela cabelereira platinada cuidadosamente ajeitada, olhos azuis, nem magra nem gorda e vestindo um longo vestido de cor azul celeste, que, com um largo e simpático sorriso, lhe dirigiu uma saudação.

- Bom dia, minha ilustre visitante, seja bem-vinda ao meu *"Canto do Repouso"*.

Ela olhou detidamente aquela simpática e amável mulher, respondeu ao cumprimento e disparou uma pergunta de uma forma que deixava claro que a queria ver respondida imediatamente:

- Afinal, amável senhora, onde está a bela vista deste *"Canto do Repouso"* que a senhora anuncia em suas placas?

A anfitriã a fitou por alguns segundos e calma e suavemente, respondeu:

- Na sua frente, minha simpática e linda visitante, na sua frente, repetiu.

Depois deste dia, que ninguém sabe e ninguém viu, ela passou a ter um comportamento tão diametralmente oposto que chegou a ficar irreconhecível para algumas pessoas que a conheciam já que tinha passado a viver de uma forma mais leve, mais suave, mais pacífica, mais tranquila, menos angustiada, menos explosiva e menos dependente de remédios para dormir.

Linda, para as inimigas

Ela levanta, toma banho e vai se vestir.

Após colocar a saia e a blusa, ela coloca os brincos nas orelhas e pergunta:

- Esse brinco ficou bem?

Ele a observa e diz:

- Ficou muito bem, aliás, eles nem eram necessários.

Ela, meio admirada com a observação dele, diz:

- Nem pensar, sem os brincos parece que estou nua.

- Acho que estás exagerando bastante, pois já estás belíssima com essa roupa e o brinco até seria dispensável.

- Tu também não gostas de te arrumar, não te importas com a tua aparência? – indagou ela.

- Sim, eu gosto de me arrumar melhor quando eu saio contigo, afinal não posso me vestir mal e eventualmente vir a te causar algum constrangimento - disse ele.

- Aliás, para mim nem precisavas te preocupar em te arrumar tanto, qualquer roupa te cai bem e sempre estarás linda.

- Muito obrigada, meu amor, eu sei que pensas assim.

- Sim, claro, eu entendo que gostas de te arrumar para as tuas amigas.

- Não, as mulheres também não se arrumam para as amigas - disse ela.

- Puxa, agora não entendi mais nada.

- Então porque as mulheres se arrumam tanto, se não é para as amigas e não é para a pessoa com quem vivem juntas?

- É para as inimigas, meu amor, para as i-ni-mi-gas!, respondeu ela acentuando cada sílaba da palavra!

Como a hora de sair já havia chegado, eles se despediram com um cuidadoso abraço para ela não amassar a roupa e, principalmente, para não macular a primorosa maquilagem e, assim, evitar que alguma "inimiga" lhe fizesse alguma observação ferina.

A menina da tapera

A menina acordou sobressaltada com o seu pequeno coração palpitando tão fortemente que lhe parecia que ia sair pela sua pequenina boca.

- Pai, mãe - chamava ela.

- O que foi, minha pequeninha? - perguntou o pai.

- Estou com muito medo.

- Medo de que? – perguntou a mãe.

- Deste barulho na parede da nossa casa – respondeu a menina.

- Não te preocupes, querida, é só o vento empurrando o nosso carrinho contra a porta da nossa casa – respondeu a mãe.

- Posso dormir na cama com vocês? – perguntou ela.

- Claro que podes, minha querida, venha - disse a mãe.

Ela saiu rapidamente da sua cama e se deitou entre os dois com os braços abertos para poder tocar em ambos e, sentindo-se protegida, dormiu logo em seguida.

Quando o sol ainda não tinha aparecido, os dois se levantaram da cama com todo o cuidado possível para não acordar a única filha deles, que ainda dormia suavemente entre os dois.

Eles eram catadores individuais de materiais recicláveis e utilizavam um carrinho que possuía duas rodas e uma barra horizontal posicionada na frente, que era utilizada para colocar o carrinho na posição horizontal para que pudesse ser puxado por essa mesma barra.

Eles eram chamados de catadores de material reciclável com utilização de veículos de tração humana, ou simplesmente, carrinheiros.

Eles precisavam sair bem cedo de casa para passar pelas ruas dos bairros próximos onde moravam para recolher o material depositado nas calçadas pelas residências e pelas empresas, que descartavam esse material reciclável por ser considerado lixo.

Era preciso madrugar, pois eles tinham que passar antes dos catadores que utilizavam camionetas ou caminhões, que, por sua vez, passavam antes do caminhão da empresa que era contratada pela prefeitura municipal para fazer a coleta dos resíduos recicláveis.

Era um mercado de trabalho bastante concorrido e quando a situação econômica do país piorava a concorrência ficava ainda mais ferrenha e, por vezes, até violenta.

Como eles saiam bem cedo, sabiam que a menina ainda estaria dormindo quando do retorno deles à casa com aquela carga preciosa, que lhes daria a renda que possibilitaria tocar a vida em frente.

Após chegarem em casa, eles separavam os materiais e os preparavam para vendê-lo para um comerciante, que, por sua vez, também fazia concorrência com os catadores motorizados e com o caminhão que recolhia o lixo em nome da prefeitura para, ao final, todos venderem para as empresas que reciclavam o lixo para reintroduzi-lo no ciclo de consumo como matéria-prima.

O casal levava uma vida muito dura, mas era o que eles conseguiam fazer após terem sido despedidos da empresa onde trabalhavam, que havia falido por não conseguir suportar a concorrência predadora que sofreu ao longo de vários anos de empresas transnacionais que assim agiam por total desídia dos governantes.

Um quase imperceptível caminho que partia do acostamento daquela imponente e importante rodovia os levava para dentro do mato onde eles haviam construído uma pequena casa de tijolos furados sem reboco com uma única peça onde dormia o casal, a filhinha deles e onde também tinham um improvisado fogão à lenha junto a uma também improvisada pia onde preparavam o ralo alimento que conseguiam obter diariamente.

A família vivia em um terreno desocupado que havia sido comprado por uma grande empresa para reserva de valor e que estava tomado pelo mato.

Ao lado dessa minúscula casa, havia uma também minúscula casinha de madeira, que continha um banco sobre um buraco onde toda a família fazia as suas necessidades fisiológicas.

De um poço abandonado que havia no terreno, eles pegavam a água para atender as necessidades da família e que também era utilizado pelos animais que viviam no mato para saciarem a sede e, em dias de muito calor, para se refrescarem.

Nesses dias de muito calor, a menina gostava de ver os pássaros voando em direção a água do poço onde se molhavam e depois voavam até o galho de uma árvore próxima para sacudir as suas assas para borrifar em todo o seu corpo a água que tinha ficado em suas penas.

Em quase todas as noites, a menina arrumava uma justificativa para amparar o pedido de ir para a cama dos pais, que sempre acabavam consentindo não sem antes de lhe falar que ela devia a se acostumar a dormir sozinha na cama dela.

Ao atingir a idade escolar, os pais levaram a menina até a escola mais próxima, que, depois de alguma relutância, aceitou receber a nova aluna, mas com a exigência de que os pais se comprometessem a informar o endereço correto da residência deles e a entregar o documento de identidade da menina.

Esse era um desafio e tanto para os pais da menina já que eles não queriam informar o local onde habitavam para evitar que essa informação pudesse eventualmente chegar à empresa proprietária do terreno que, certamente, viria desalojá-los.

Quanto ao documento de identidade, também foi uma decisão importante a ser tomada, pois eles, com todas as agruras que já haviam passado com as autoridades constituídas, entendiam que era melhor que a filha fosse uma pessoa invisível e um documento de identidade só serviria para constar de um cadastro oficial que facilitava o trabalho das autoridades quando precisavam fazer alguma investigação.

Aquela máxima de que a corda sempre rebenta no ponto mais fraco os fazia temer de participar de qualquer cadastro oficial.

- Acho melhor não tirar esse tal de documento — disse o marido para a esposa.

- Mas a nossa filha precisa aprender, pelo menos a ler e a fazer contas - ponderou a esposa.

- Afinal, continuou a esposa, quando ela crescer, ela também será catadora e precisará saber ler na porta do depósito qual o tipo de material que o proprietário compra além de precisar conhecer os números para ter certeza de que o dono do depósito está lhe pagando corretamente.

- Tens razão, minha esposa, amanhã vamos ver como se faz esse tal documento.

- Mas, disse ele, vamos dizer que moramos naquela invasão onde está instalado o depósito que nos compra o material que coletamos.

Eles escolheram um dia da semana em que a coleta era mais fraca e foram às autoridades e explicaram que a menina havia nascido em casa e que não sabiam que precisavam registrá-la o que ficaram sabendo somente agora quando foram matriculá-la na escola do bairro.

Pediram para a autoridade desculpá-los por não terem nem conta de água, nem conta de luz para comprovar o endereço, mas eles garantiram que moravam naquela invasão que, por sinal, era bastante conhecida das autoridades, pois lá moravam várias centenas de pessoas que se abrigavam em barracos muitas vezes feitos com superpostas camadas de pedaços de papelão.

Com o documento em mãos e com aquele falso endereço, foram à escola para cumprir o compromisso assumido com a professora.

Iniciadas as aulas, a menina ficou bem entusiasmada ao começar a aprender a relacionar as letras com os seus respectivos sons.

Ao mostrar para os pais o resultado do aprendizado, todos ficaram muito felizes e, nesta noite, a menina não pediu para passar para a cama deles.

Ao ter início o aprendizado de juntar as letras, na etapa que é chamada de silábica, a alegria da menina começou a desaparecer.

A professora escreveu no quadro a frase vovô viu a uva e à medida que a professora avançava na explicação mais o medo da menina aumentava, pois não conseguia entender o significado daquilo que estava escrito no quadro.

Ela até conhecia as letras das palavras que a professora tinha escrito no quadro, pois ela já as tinha relacionado com alguma coisa que fazia parte do mundo dela.

O "v" ela havia relacionado com os paus que sustentavam o telhado da casa, o "o" ela havia relacionado com o pneu do carrinho do pai, o "a" ela havia relacionado com a chaleira sem alça e sem tampa da mãe, o "u" ela havia relacionado com a pia da cozinha e o "i" com a chaminé de uma casa que ela via à distância.

- Basta eu decorar essas figuras e juntá-las para escrever a frase - pensou a menina.

- Mas o que significam essas palavras e o que adianta eu saber ler e escrever, mas não saber o que está escrito – continuou pensando a menina.

- E ela, apavorada, se indagava: - o que será que é vovô? - o que será que é uva?

O fato de não saber o significado dessas palavras, passou a lhe causar uma angústia tal que ela não mais conseguia ouvir as explicações da professora.

E a angústia dela aumentava ainda mais quando ela notava que todas as crianças não só demonstravam saber o significado daquelas palavras como também todas abriam largos sorrisos ao pronunciá-las.

Ela nunca tinha ouvido a palavra uva e muito menos a palavra vovô.

Naquele dia, ela voltou para casa decidida a dizer para os pais que não queria mais ir para a escola, pois não queria passar a vergonha de ter de solicitar para a professora o significado daquelas palavras que ela sabia ler, escrever e pronunciar, mas não sabia o que aquelas palavras significavam.

Depois de muito pensar, ela resolveu falar com os pais sobre essa dificuldade que ela estava passando na escola e perguntou para eles o que significavam a palavra vovô e a palavra uva.

Ensinar o significado da palavra uva era fácil, pois eles já tinham visto essa fruta, mas eles sentiram um enorme peso caindo sobre as suas cabeças para ter de explicar o significado da palavra vovô.

Mas, não tinha alternativa, teriam que falar para a pequeninha sobre a história da família de ambos.

Após os relatos, um mutismo total marcou a convivência dos três por vários dias.

Os pais com vergonha do passado deles e a menina magoada pelo fato de os seus pais nunca terem lhe falado que ela tinha tido uma família maior, mas que todos haviam morrido pelas sucessivas infecções provocadas pela desnutrição e pela falta de higiene.

Dia após dia os pais saiam para a coleta do material reciclável totalmente atormentados e a menina, cada vez mais cabisbaixa, ia para a escola muito a contragosto.

Ela tinha vontade de sumir.

Ela não sentia mais vontade de viver.

Naquela manhã em que os pais saíram para o rotineiro trabalho, o dia estava com uma forte neblina o que lhes transmitia um forte desejo de ficar em casa junto com a filha que continuava dormindo.

Mas precisavam sair e recolher o material, pois, afinal, eles contavam com aquele dinheiro ganho diariamente para o sustento deles.

O marido saiu puxando o carinho e a esposa se deitou sobre o assoalho feito de pedaços de madeira e de latas enferrujadas e se protegeu com um velho e rasgado cobertor que ela havia recolhido no dia anterior.

Absorto em pensamentos, o marido, como fazia diariamente, equilibrava e puxava o carrinho de duas rodas pelo acostamento da rodovia quando, de repente, eles sentiram uma forte batida no carrinho que os jogou na sarjeta da rodovia.

Enquanto eles se recuperavam do susto e dos ferimentos, viram um jovem homem corpulento, com volumosos músculos nas pernas e nos braços, vindo na direção deles.

- Olha o que vocês fizeram com o meu carro, seus imprestáveis - esbravejou o jovem bem-vestido e com aparência de pessoa rica.

- Mas, moço, nos desculpe, por favor, nós estávamos no acostamento indo na mesma direção do senhor e não vimos o seu carro chegar.

- Então, seus imprestáveis, vocês querem dizer que a culpa é minha?

- Que absurdo, vocês nem podiam estar na rodovia - continuou, cada vez mais exaltado, o jovem motorista.

- Mas, doutor, nós estamos trabalhando para sustentar a nossa família.

- Trabalhando? E vocês chamam isso de trabalho, seus vagabundos!

- Sim, nós estamos trabalhando, sim senhor, e o senhor não pode nos chamar de vagabundos – disse a esposa, intervindo na discussão

- Afinal, disse ela, nós recolhemos o lixo de vocês e o nosso trabalho, além de nos dar uma pequeníssima renda, deixa um mundo bem mais limpo para todos nós.

- Ora, que conversa mais boba é essa! - exclamou o jovem motorista.

- Vocês recolhem lixo porque não têm méritos, se vocês tivessem méritos, vocês não precisariam estar recolhendo lixo.

- Mas, doutor, nós só estamos nesse trabalho porque perdemos o nosso emprego pela falência da empresa onde trabalhávamos.

- Mas se vocês tivessem mérito, vocês já teriam arrumado outro emprego - respondeu o jovem com aparência d abastado.

- Mas moço, o senhor é tão jovem e já tem esse carro, e, pela sua aparência, parece que é muito rico, foi por seus próprios méritos ou foi porque o senhor ganhou uma herança dos seus pais? - respondeu a mulher.

Neste momento, o corpulento motorista se enfureceu ainda mais e levantou o braço para dar um tapa naquela mulher que tinha tido a ousadia de enfrentá-lo.

Ao ver o movimento do braço do homem, o marido se interpôs entre ele e a esposa para evitar que a violência física viesse a se somar àquela dispensável e inútil violência verbal.

- Ora veja só, estás querendo me enfrentar, vagabundo petulante?

- Não, eu só quero evitar que o doutor bata na minha esposa - respondeu o marido.

Nesse momento, fora de si, o jovem deu um passo para trás, sacou uma brilhante arma da sua cintura e descarregou toda a munição nos dois, que tombaram sobre uma enorme poça de seus próprios sangues.

Durante todo esse tempo, vários outros carros e caminhões passaram na rodovia, mas resolviam ir adiante, pois só viam um carro parado, um jovem homem bem-vestido e um carrinho de catador de lixo quebrado.

Os motoristas dos carros e caminhões que passavam não viam o casal, pois ele era formado de pessoas que não eram vistas, eles faziam parte do grupo social dos socialmente invisíveis.

Quando o dia clareou, a polícia chegou e algumas pessoas que também caminhavam diariamente pelo acostamento da rodovia indicaram onde o casal morava e a escola onde a menina estudava.

A escola foi avisada e as professoras foram até a casa onde a menina continuava esperando os pais chegarem com o resultado do trabalho do dia.

Após o sepultamento dos pais em uma cova rasa do município, por um tempo pessoas caridosas foram levando semanalmente mantimentos e agasalhos para ajudar a menina órfã a sobreviver.

Mas isso não bastava, pois a menina não tinha condições, nem força e nem conhecimento para manter a casa, que acabou virando uma quase tapera e decidiu, determinada:

– Eu preciso trabalhar para ter um pouco de renda.

Além disso, ao continuar o trabalho dos pais ela sentiria a presença deles e isso ajudaria a fortalecê-la.

Mesmo com pouca força e com pouco conhecimento, mas contando com a compreensão e um pequeno apoio dos colegas de trabalho, ela passou a trabalhar na mesma atividade e no mesmo trajeto dos seus pais.

As pessoas com quem ela convivia durante o trabalho de coleta de materiais recicláveis e conheciam o drama da menina passaram a respeitá-la e a chamá-la carinhosamente de a menina da tapera.

Tanto na ida para o trabalho quanto na volta para casa ela utilizava o acostamento da rodovia, mas sempre no sentido contrário ao dos carros e caminhões, pois, em assim agindo, ela pensava que evitaria acidentes como o que resultou na morte dos seus pais, já que ela sempre poderia ver os veículos que vinham em sua direção.

Dias, semanas e anos se passaram e a menina da tapera ficou adolescente e chamava a atenção não só dos colegas de trabalho como também dos motoristas, das pessoas que depositavam o lixo na calçada e dos transeuntes.

Em poucos momentos de desconcentração a que ela se permitia, ela jogava bola com os colegas e impressionava pela habilidade com que ela dominava a bola de futebol.

Em um destes momentos, havia um grande congestionamento de veículos na rodovia e muitos motoristas ficaram observando a menina a jogar e quando ela se retirou da brincadeira muitos abriram os vidros dos carros e a aplaudiram.

Além da habilidade com a bola de futebol, a menina da tapera chamava a atenção pela sua beleza física e pela tenacidade que demonstrava ao enfrentar o seu árduo trabalho.

Mas, o que mais chamava a atenção, principalmente dos seus colegas de trabalho, era a profunda tristeza que expressava no seu semblante e, em especial, nos seus olhos.

Ela não conseguia sorrir nem em momentos de desconcentração e nem diante de situações ou falas engraçadas.

Ela sentia muito a falta dos pais e quando pensava neles sentia uma profunda, demorada e quase insuportável angústia, que lhe provocava dor e sensação de aperto no peito e na garganta.

Numa noite, ao voltar para casa com o carinho vazio e com alguns poucos trocados no bolso fruto do trabalho daquele dia, ela caminhava, como sempre fazia, pelo acostamento no sentido contrário ao dos carros quando viu ao longe duas luzes brancas e extremamente brilhantes.

As luzes eram tão brilhantes e tão lindas que lhe ofuscaram a visão, mas que lhe transmitiram uma sensação de grande alegria, pois pareciam aquelas luzes que diziam ser própria dos anjos.

Naquele momento, ela viu naquelas luzes a figura dos seus pais deitados na cama.

- Pai, mãe - gritou ela.

- O que foi, minha pequeninha? – ela ouviu o pai perguntar.

- Posso dormir na cama com vocês? – perguntou ela.

- Claro que podes, minha querida, venha - ela ouviu a mãe dizer.

Extasiada, ela largou o carinho, abriu os braços e correu em direção ao ponto que ficava no centro daquelas luzes brilhantes para poder tocar no seu pai e na sua mãe no mesmo momento e se deitar entre eles na cama onde eles estavam deitados, exatamente como ela fazia quando era criança.

No encontro, o carro jogou a menina da tapera para os ares e ela, em vez de dor, sentiu uma agradável sensação de estar voando e o sangue que a encobria lhe transmitiu um calor tão agradável que se assemelhava ao calor da cama dos pais.

Quando o corpo da menina da tapera caiu sobre o asfalto molhado com o seu próprio sangue ele já não tinha mais vida, mas a linda e brilhante luz do espírito da menina da tapera encontrava as luzes lindas e brilhantes dos espíritos dos seus queridos e amados pais.

Dia da mulher

Os dois se encontraram na mesma mesa do bar onde sempre se reuniam no final da tarde para tomar um café, uma água e conversar sobre o dia a dia deles e da sociedade em que viviam.

- Ei, já mandastes as felicitações para as mulheres pelo dia delas? – pergunta o mais velho.

- Eu não mandei nada, afinal essa é mais uma data meramente comercial.

- Esquece disso e manda, pois elas sabem que é uma data comercial, mas, como nós, elas também gostam de serem lembradas.

- Certo, concordo.

O mais jovem, parou e escreveu em seu smartphone:

"Mulheres, eu as reverencio todos os dias, pois sou, espontânea e convictamente, um eterno dependente de vocês."

"Queiram, por favor, receber meus respeitosos beijos diários."

- Que tal, ficou bom? perguntou o mais jovem.

- Sim, melhor do que nada. – disse o mais velho.

Despedindo-se com um "até a próxima", ambos saíram.

Ferro velho

- FÉÉÉÉRRO VÉÉÉÉLHOOOO ♫

- COMPRO OSSO E VIDRO QUEBRADO ♫
- JORNAL VELHO E REVISTA VELHA ♫
- FERRO VELHO E FOGÃO VELHO ♫

- FÉÉÉÉRRO VÉÉÉÉLHOOOO ♫

Com voz alta e com uma melodia própria, o velho homem desdentado seguia a pé ao lado de sua carroça e anunciava a sua atividade de comprador de material reciclável.

Para minimizar os efeitos da sua surdez, ele colocava a mão esquerda em forma de concha sobre o ouvido criando uma espécie de caixa de ressonância que amplificava o som de sua voz, e, com isso, conseguia modular a altura da própria voz.

Com a mão direita ele segurava as rédeas que dirigiam um velho e alquebrado cavalo, que tracionava aquela velha carroça lotada de compras que eram colocados no assoalho da carroça e em uns paus verticais que outrora suportavam um toldo de lona.

Assim, aquele harmônico conjunto formado pelo velho, pelo cavalo e pela carroça se movia pelas ruas de chão batido, cheias de buracos e com tortuosos valos por onde escorriam a água da chuva e o esgoto das casas.

Eram tempos de grande escassez que se seguiam após o término da guerra que havia destruído grande parte da economia do país.

O esforço financeiro feito pelo governo para sustentar a guerra havia quebrado grande parte das empresas e as que restavam só sobreviveram por terem tido a oportunidade de modificar as suas operações para produzir e comercializar equipamentos e insumos para a guerra.

Tão logo terminou a guerra, essas mesmas empresas passaram a se dedicar ao processamento de produtos recicláveis, que atendiam minimamente as necessidades da população, como aquelas que utilizam sucata de ferro para produzir vergalhões necessários para a reconstrução de prédios que haviam sido destruídos ou por ação militar ou por falta de manutenção.

Grande parte da economia estava destroçada, mas uma pequena parte da economia estava pujante, pois a guerra é isso: muitos perdem tudo ou quase tudo e poucos ganham muito seja pela apropriação da riqueza dos mortos e fugitivos, seja pelo fornecimento de insumos e equipamentos para a destruição e no fim da guerra fornecendo insumos e equipamentos para a reconstrução dos países que serviram de palco para o confronto bélico.

Aliás, todas as guerras têm como motor principal o desejo de expropriação de riquezas alheias.

O menino aproveitava a passagem do *"velho do ferro velho"* para vender restos que ele recolhia durante a semana em terrenos baldios.

Em algumas semanas as buscas, que incluíam pequenas escavações, rendiam mais e em outras nem tanto, mas, com essa atividade, ele colaborava com as rendas da pequena família que passava por dificuldades decorrentes da guerra.

Em um desses dias, ele achou várias xícaras de louça que estavam enterradas em um terreno muito úmido e quando ele conseguiu desenterrá-las elas vieram cheias de barro.

Pensou em limpá-las, mas parou e pensou que poderia colocar as xícaras de vidro cheias de barro embaixo dos cacos de vidros e esperar que o velho não se apercebesse e assim ele aumentaria o rendimento da semana vendendo barro por vidro.

O velho pesava o material em uma pequena balança manual que tinha em uma extremidade uma argola onde ele colocava o dedo indicador para segurá-la e na outra extremidade havia um gancho onde ele pendurava os objetos a serem adquiridos e no meio havia uma mola que movimentava um indicador sobre uma peça que indicava o peso dos materiais.

Como essa mola estava bastante enferrujada ela precisava de mais peso para se movimentar e isso fazia com que a balança marcasse sempre menos peso que o real e era esse proceder do velho que dava a justificava para o menino tentar vender barro por vidro.

Naquele dia, enquanto aguardava o *"velho do ferro velho"* passar, a tensão do menino aumentava a cada minuto que passava, pois ele não tinha certeza se estava procedendo corretamente.

Ao ver a carroça ao longe o coração do menino disparou e as suas faces ficaram extremamente ruborizadas.

Devia entregar barro por vidro? Não devia? A balança enferrujada justificava a atitude dele?

O velho parou a carroça e passou a pesar o material que menino lhe oferecia e ao pegar o saco dos vidros vasculhou tudo e retirou as xicaras cheias de barro e, sem dizer nada, as jogou na sarjeta.

O menino perguntou: - o que houve, o senhor não quer as xicaras?

- Ora, garoto, não queira me fazer de bobo me entregando barro em vez de vidro, disse o velho.

- Me desculpe, senhor, eu não havia me dado conta disso, mas só um momento que eu tiro o barro de dentro e lhe entrego elas vazias.

- Eu não tenho tempo para perder, garoto, respondeu o velho e, pagando o material que havia aceitado voltou a caminhar pela rua a fora.

Os meses se sucederam e a rotina semanal da passagem da carroça e a venda do material que o menino encontrava continuou normalmente.

Em um dia o menino encontrou num terreno tomado por um espesso mato uma peça que ele percebia que fora fabricada com metais diferentes e que continha várias pedras encravadas e que brilhavam intensamente.

Puxa, pensou o menino, isso deve valer mais que o peso da peça.

Mostrou a peça para alguns vizinhos mais idosos e todos eles concordaram que a peça devia valer bem mais que o peso, mas não podiam ter certeza já que não entendiam nada sobre peças antigas.

- Pergunte para o *"velho do ferro velho"*, todos disseram, afinal ele trabalha com isso e deve entender ou poderá levar para alguém que entenda e possa avaliar essa peça.

O menino ficou pensativo por várias semanas e sempre ficava em dúvida se devia ou não mostrar para o velho aquele seu achado.

Mas não havia outro jeito, afinal o *"velho do ferro velho"* era o único que passava pela rua dele que poderia entender do assunto.

Naquela semana ao ver a carroça apontar no início da rua, o coração do menino disparou, pois ele havia decidido mostrar o seu achado para o velho.

- Bom dia, meu caro senhor, eu quero lhe mostrar isso que encontrei e gostaria que o senhor me dissesse o quanto isso vale, pois, me parece, que ela deve valer mais que o próprio peso, afinal ela é tão bonita - exclamou o menino.

O velho, sem falar nada, pegou a peça analisou-a detidamente e disse:

- Olha garoto, eu não sei se isso vale mais do que o peso dela – disse o velho.

- Mas, continuou o velho, eu vou lhe pagar o peso dela em ferro e na próxima semana se eu conseguir revendê-la por um preço melhor eu te dou alguma coisa a mais.

- Pode ser assim? – perguntou o velho.

- Pode, claro, caro senhor, até a próxima semana, disse o menino.

O velho pegou a balança enferrujada, pesou a peça e pagou ao menino o valor correspondente ao peso de ferro e partiu.

Durante toda a semana, o menino não conseguiu dormir e quando pegava no sono sonhava que estava ouvindo a voz do velho anunciando a chegada.

No dia da passagem do *"velho do ferro velho"*, o menino acordou na madrugada e, como não conseguia dormir, foi para a beira da rua e ficou aguardando o tão sonhado cântico do velho.

As horas passavam e, a cada minuto, ele sempre pensava em estar ouvindo o cântico do velho, mas o harmonioso conjunto do velho, do cavalo e da carroça não aparecia.

O conjunto, não apareceu naquela semana e nem nas outras que se sucederam.

Os anos se passaram e nunca mais o *"velho do ferro velho"* apareceu.

E o menino ficou velho sonhando todas as noites com aquele cântico que tinha ouvido por tanto tempo:

- FÉÉÉÉRRO VÉÉÉÉLHOOOO ♫

- COMPRO OSSO E VIDRO QUEBRADO ♫
- JORNAL VELHO E REVISTA VELHA ♫
- FERRO VELHO E FOGÃO VELHO ♫

- FÉÉÉÉRRO VÉÉÉÉLHOOOO ♫

As pirâmides sociais

Eles se encontram nos mais requintados e exclusivos clubes de golfe, em estações privadas de esqui, em paradisíacas ilhas particulares e em exclusivíssimos aeroportos onde não há controles, em especial os aduaneiros e migratórios.

Nestes locais, eles podem conversar à vontade e ficam livres para praticar todas as atividades que lhe vierem à mente, inclusive as que são consideradas severas transgressões sociais insuscetíveis de indulgências para os ricos, remediados, pobres e miseráveis.

E são nestes grupos, habitantes de outras pirâmides sociais, que são selecionadas, investigadas, testadas e examinadas as pessoas que lhes prestam serviços a troco de, para as pessoas prestadoras, considerada régia remuneração, e, para eles, os pagadores, apenas pequena fração de valores da renda que recebem em frações de segundos.

Os critérios para recrutar as pessoas prestadoras são rigorosos e não importa em qual das pirâmides sociais elas vivem, mas devem atender exigências fundamentais como a da absoluta lealdade e a da total discrição.

Afinal, pensam os pagadores, poder ingressar na pirâmide social deles deve ser considerado para as prestadoras como um privilégio, uma visita a um outro planeta onde só moram deuses e deusas.

Eles não se dão conta de serem - prestadoras e pagadores - pessoas idênticas quanto às necessidades humanas essenciais que são as necessidades fisiológicas de amar, respirar, dormir, comer, beber, mijar e cagar e que todas essas necessidades precisam ser atendidas por todos, pois quando uma delas, apenas uma, deixa de funcionar adequadamente qualquer habitante de qualquer pirâmide social fica em risco de morte.

Também não se dão conta de que essas necessidades essenciais, que colocam todos em absoluta condição de igualdade, fazem com que todas as pirâmides desapareçam e se transformem em uma única linha rasa, reta, infinita, ilimitada e sem interrupção, que, dada a curvatura da terra, acaba se transformando em um grande círculo de pontos unidos e iguais.

Em certa ocasião, eles, os da exclusivíssima pirâmide social onde habitam algumas centenas de famílias, após os deleites que aquele momento lhes proporcionava, conversavam sobre negócios e sobre como deveriam proceder para manter aquela situação social exclusiva e como proceder para acumular mais riqueza, que continuaria lhes proporcionando aqueles momentos únicos.

Sim, eles falam abertamente sobre os seus negócios, pois eles mantêm atividades complementares que formam enormes e impenetráveis oligopólios.

Com o encontro chegando ao final, o decano falou:

- Meus caros confrades, devido à presença de alguns jovens herdeiros, precisamos relembrar duas das grandes teses que amparam os nossos ganhos e que, por isso, precisam ser constantemente robustecidas junto às sociedades em que atuamos.

E passou a explicar rapidamente essas duas teses.

- A primeira, é a tese de que o Estado deve ser administrado como uma empresa privada.

-Essa tem uma explicação bem simples: como o caixa da empresa é o bolso do dono, o caixa do Estado passa a ser o bolso do detentor do poder efetivo, do poder real.

- Para tanto, precisamos continuar elegendo pessoas que não se preocupem em administrar a coisa pública em benefício dos eleitores, mas administrá-la para continuar entregando o Estado para nós, os financiadores, administrarmos.

- É sempre necessário lembrar, que a condição de detentores do poder real, do poder efetivo, nos possibilita acumular cada vez mais riqueza pessoal, que é justamente o que nos proporciona a captura dos administradores eleitos.

- Portanto, é fundamental que nós, os financiadores, deixemos de lado quaisquer impulsos de atender pedidos de melhor distribuição de renda entre as pessoas de todas as pirâmides sociais e, no máximo, até para poder mantermos a nossa posição, podemos concordar em melhorar a distribuição de renda entre as pessoas das demais pirâmides sociais, mas nunca envolvendo a nossa.

- Que eles lá se entendam, mas nós temos que ficar fora disso sempre.

- Aliás, é preciso manter neles também a ideia, a ilusão, de que há apenas uma pirâmide social, o que cria a falsa perspectiva da ascensão social até o sonhado topo.

- Para tanto, precisamos manter a nossa pirâmide totalmente invisível e, para isso, temos que evitar exposições em qualquer tipo de mídia, ou seja, meus caros, as normais disputas de vaidades que ocorrem entre nós devem ficar absolutamente restritas ao nosso círculo.

E continuou o decano.

- A segunda, é a tese de que o espírito animal do empreendedor deve ser sempre deixado totalmente livre.

-Essa também tem uma explicação bem simples: ficando totalmente livres, nós podemos continuar com o comportamento dos animais que atacam para saciar a fome, com ferocidade aumentada em época de seca, mas que também ataca para manter e alargar o território sob seu domínio.

- Autorizados ou desautorizados pela lei, o que em muitos países não faz a menor diferença, pois tem a lei que pega, a que não pega ou a que pega de forma seletiva, devemos sempre buscar mais riqueza, custe o que custar, pois esta, a fortuna, é a medida utilizada para estabelecer a altura a ser ocupada na nossa exclusivíssima pirâmide social.

- Afinal, as outras classes sociais, encharcadas de infindáveis necessidades de consumo e de explosivas alegrias, bem como as pequenas e médias empresas, que sustentam os sindicatos, associações, federações e confederações, sem tempo para se dedicarem a conhecer a coisa pública, são facilmente convencidas a nos dar razão, os detentores do poder real.

- Mantendo sempre vivas estas duas teses, conseguimos produzir dois Estados com códigos bem distintos: um que se deteriora dia após dia e o outro que se alimenta dessa deterioração e se fortalece dia após dia.

E continuou, com voz firme.

- É preciso manter essa ordem totalitária que usa métodos ferozes para poder manter o amplo extrativismo, que carreia para as nossas holdings familiares a renda e o prestígio, que são os grandes mantenedores do nosso modo de viver.

- Continuemos sendo pragmáticos, para nós não há polaridades, nem multi, nem bi, nem unipolaridade, pois sempre vamos financiar fortemente todos os lados e todas as pontas e ganhe quem ganhar nós continuaremos no comando, pois os financiados são como a água, que se molda e se ajusta a toda e qualquer forma e condição.

- Precisamos continuar comandando informalmente os que detém o poder formal, pois são eles que comandam os exércitos e as polícias, que com suas capacidades bélicas, armas e inteligências são os garantidores últimos de todo o sistema.

E continuou o decano.

- É importante frisar que além do comando da força, são eles, os eleitos, que autorizam e regulam todas as atividades econômicas legislando sobre a concentração de mercados, as fusões e incorporações, os monopólios, os oligopólios, a exploração do solo e do subsolo, o trânsito mundial de pessoas e de mercadorias, a concorrência, o mercado financeiro, a utilização de novas tecnologias e de novos softwares, as plataformas multifacetadas, as comunicações, a internet, e todas as políticas que nos proporcionam o exercício do real, do efetivo, poder.

- Quando as populações começam a sentir a falta de governo e a reclamar da ausência de políticas públicas, devemos providenciar para que algumas de nossas empresas iniciem movimentos para minimizar essas ausências providenciando campanhas que visem substituir os governos.

- Assim, teremos um duplo ganho: o de diminuir a importância dos governos e o de possibilitar a implementação de algum serviço que nos permita, direta ou indiretamente, acumular mais riqueza.

- Um bom exemplo disso é o que fizemos quando começam as reclamações sobre a deficiência do ensino público onde sempre apresentamos como solução o financiamento de cursos "modernos" para governantes que, sub-repticiamente, sempre defendem a adoção de modelos educacionais que tragam embutida a validação da nossa ideologia.

- Portanto, meus caros jovens, a acumulação da riqueza material é fundamental para termos o efetivo exercício desse poder absoluto.

Falando de forma mais libidinosa ainda, continuou.

- E o poder, meus jovens, o exercício pleno do real poder, do efetivo poder, do poder absoluto é o que nos possibilita aquilo que nos satisfaz, aquilo que faz sentido em nossas vidas e o que nos coloca em êxtase, em embevecimento, em encantamento e em endeusação.

E finalizou dando a voz de comando.

- Não podemos permitir que as populações derrubem a nossa agenda de falsas democracia e liberdade e que eles, os membros das outras pirâmides sociais, consigam eleger pessoas que tornem efetivas tanto a democracia quanto a liberdade e queiram nos submeter aos seus comandos.

Combinando que as próximas reuniões do grupo continuariam sendo agendadas pelos conhecidos canais próprios, seguros e exclusivos, se despediram com cumpliciosos abraços.

Após a saída da ilha de todos os pagadores em seus flamantes jatos, um grupo das pessoas prestadoras embarca em um pequeno iate que os levaria de volta ao continente.

Durante a viagem, absortas, observavam as brancas nuvens, os raios do sol e o vai e vem das ondas, dos pássaros e dos peixes.

Já longe, bem longe dos olhos e dos ouvidos dos feitores que os comandavam, algumas delas começaram a divagar.

- Eita, eu vi aquele mais jovem não conseguindo respirar direito, cheguei a ficar com pena.

- Vixe, eu vi aquele mais velho tendo uma crise urinária que chegou a dar dó.

- Oxente, eu vi aquele mais alto e atlético ajoelhado em frente ao vaso sanitário - aquele branco que tinha detalhes em ouro, explicou — tendo pavorosos espasmos estomacais, que lhe provocavam contínuos jorros de vômitos.

- Bah! eu ouvi aqueles dois mais jovens confessando um ao outro que estavam passando por uma profunda depressão, um por ter morrido o seu animal de estimação e o outro por ter brigado com a namorada.

Quando todos se calaram e voltaram a sentir a natureza que as envolvia, uma quinta pessoa, mais introspectiva, cofiando o cabelo com a mão direita apoiou o queixo sobre a mão esquerda e balbuciou:

- Pois é, no essencial, todos somos iguais.

Mulher bonita

Mulher bonita
é tautologia,
é pleonasmo,
é redundância.

Pois, a mulher ...
sempre será bela,
sempre será linda,
sempre será bonita,
sempre será distinta,
sempre será formosa,
sempre será elegante,
sempre será classuda,
sempre será agradável,
sempre será maravilhosa!

Lembranças eternas

Os omissos,
os covardes,
os traidores,,
os coniventes,
os entreguistas,
os colaboracionistas,
serão a ferro e fogo ... marcados,
serão eternamente ... lembrados!

Herança

Caminhando ao léu pela mesma rua, eles se encontram.

- Olá, disse ela, sorridente e alegre.

- Oi, há quanto tempo não nos vemos, disse ele, demonstrando satisfação pelo encontro.

- É bem verdade, amigo, então que tal aproveitarmos essa agradável causalidade para conversarmos descontraidamente como nos velhos tempos?

- Bela ideia, amiga, podemos ir naquele mesmo boteco aonde sempre íamos.

Chegando, eles escolheram uma mesa ao fundo do salão onde gostavam de sentar-se para conversar com mais tranquilidade e para observar o movimento do entra e sai dos fregueses, a correria dos garçons e o olhar de controle da pessoa que ficava no caixa.

Era um final de tarde primaveril, que apetecia uma boa conversa e uma bebida.

- Vamos tomar um vinho? - perguntou ele.

- Eu prefiro ficar com o outro produto da uva, respondeu ela sorrindo, e completou, prefiro um suco de uva.

- Mas, disse ele, dizem que o vinho é saudável e que deveríamos tomar um cálice todos os dias por eles conterem componentes que lhes conferem propriedades que fazem bem à saúde das pessoas.

- Pois então, respondeu ela, a principal diferença, a diferença fundamental, entre o suco da uva e o vinho é a de que o vinho tem álcool, que, comprovadamente, pode vir a ser muito prejudicial à saúde, já que ele pode gerar dependência, portanto se o vinho tem componentes saudáveis então o suco da uva também os tem.

- Dizem, acrescentou ela, que isso se verifica especialmente com as uvas escuras, mas, sendo verdade ou não, eu sempre prefiro tomar o suco, seja ele de uma uva escura ou de outra cor qualquer, pois ele, como tem processo de produção bem diferente da do vinho, com certeza não contém álcool.

- Perfeito, concordou ele, como sempre, tuas opiniões sobre esse tema são sempre bem fundamentadas e incontestáveis, vamos aos sucos, então.

Ambos pediram um suco de uva escura ao garçom e seguiram conversando.

- Sabes que foi muito bom eu ter te encontrado com disponibilidade para conversar – disse ela -, pois estou com algumas dúvidas emocionais e existenciais e sempre gostei muito de ouvir as tuas opiniões porque em várias oportunidades me auxiliastes a colocar os pés no chão mesmo que, às vezes, as tuas colocações fossem um tanto duras demais.

- Opa, muito obrigado, amiga, me dás uma grande satisfação em permitires que eu possa tentar te auxiliar em qualquer coisa que estejas necessitando, mas, pelo que entendi, o assunto é bem íntimo e esse local, por ser um ambiente público, não me parece adequado para conversarmos sobre isso, então acho que a gente devia escolher outro local e um outro momento.

- Tens razão, disse ela, mas, como hoje a minha angústia chegou no limite do insuportável, eu gostaria de desabafar logo contigo e, se isso não te causar nenhum transtorno, poderíamos ir agora até o meu apartamento.

- Sim, com certeza, podemos ir, minha cara amiga, afinal terei enorme prazer em retornar ao teu apartamento onde já passamos bons momentos juntos.

Assim, eles pagaram as respectivas contas e saíram calmamente em direção ao apartamento dela, que ficava bem próximo do local onde estavam.

- Então, minha cara amiga, o que está te deixando tão angustiada?

- Pois então, disse ela, estou com um problema de saúde que está me deixando bastante chateada e até um pouco revoltada.

- Opa, exclamou ele, explica melhor isso, pois agora me deixastes mais preocupado ainda.

Nesse momento, encontraram alguns antigos amigos, pararam, conversaram, se despediram e seguiram, em silêncio, rumo ao apartamento dela.

Chegando ao edifício, entraram no elevador e se mantiveram calados, pois outras pessoas entraram junto com eles no elevador.

Seguindo a antiga rotina, entraram no apartamento, deixaram os calçados no vestíbulo, se dirigiram à cozinha, pegaram copos de água e se dirigiram até a sala onde se sentaram, um em cada ponta do mesmo sofá de três lugares.

- Pois bem, amiga, o que está acontecendo com a tua saúde? É muito grave? Me deixastes nervoso com o que me dissestes.

- Pois então, amigo, há pouco tempo comecei a ter uma complicação física e consultei vários especialistas, que, após vários exames clínicos, não encontraram nada que justificasse a existência da tal complicação e essa situação está me deixando cada vez mais ansiosa, mais angustiada, pois não sei o que fazer, estou totalmente perdida.

- Mas, demonstrando forte nervosismo ele disparou uma série de perguntas, os especialistas não chegaram a nenhuma conclusão? não encontram nem uma pista qualquer sobre ela? não disseram nada que pudesse haver, pelo menos, um pequeno ponto de convergência entre eles?

- Sim, respondeu ela, essa é a questão central, pois o ponto de convergência foi a tal herança genética.

E continuou.

- Todos eles fizeram várias especulações, apontaram para várias possibilidades, mas reconheciam que não tinham muita certeza sobre nenhuma delas e que, diante do meu quadro pessoal e familiar, o mais provável seria a existência de um problema genético para o qual não há tratamento médico disponível.

- Bem, minha amiga, parafraseando um ditado muito popular, eu te diria que "o *que não tem solução, solucionado está*", portanto, amiga, vais ter de aceitar a situação e deixar essa angústia toda de lado.

- Aliás, continuou ele, estás complicando as coisas para ti mesma, pois estás te colocando dentro de uma situação absurdamente paradoxal.

- Como assim? – perguntou ela.

- Veja, respondeu ele, tens uma complicação que ninguém pode resolver e essa situação está te deixando angustiada, no entanto, estás colocando a tua saúde, que tanto prezas, em risco ao contrair de forma espontânea uma nova doença.

- Não entendi, disse ela.

- Acontece que o estado de angústia sempre causa problemas bem sérios para qualquer pessoa, portanto, minha amiga, me desculpe, mas essa tua reação me parece demonstrar uma atitude fortemente masoquista.

- Opa, amigo, não precisas pegar tão pesado assim.

- Me desculpe, amiga, mas essa tua atitude não faz o menor sentido, pois, como ninguém consegue resolver essa tua complicação, em vez de te resignares com ela tu estás contraindo espontaneamente mais uma complicação, que, certamente, vai produzir várias outras complicações para a tua saúde.

- Sim, tens razão, mas essa coisa de herança genética me incomoda muito o que me faz ficar com uma certa raiva dos meus pais, entendes?

- Opa, claro que entendo e esse é um assunto sobre o qual podemos fazer um excelente debate, mas antes eu vou buscar mais água.

Na volta da cozinha, ele continuou.

- Tens um belo apartamento, é grande, está finamente decorado, está situado num bairro nobre da cidade o que demonstra que o teu padrão de vida está muito acima da média da nossa população.

- Obrigado, respondeu ela.

E ele continuou.

- Tens alguém que te ajuda na faxina dele?

- Sim, tenho, responde ela.

- Que ótimo, além disso tudo, és muito bonita, és muito inteligente, és uma mulher classuda, tens o porte de uma mulher poderosa, tens lindos olhos, tens lindos cabelos e as feições do teu rosto são as que muitas mulheres gostariam de ter.

Meio encabulada, ela o interrompeu.

- Menos, menos, amigo não é para tudo isso, mas, de qualquer forma, agradeço os teus elogios.

- Não foram elogios, amiga, apenas fiz um relato das tuas características físicas, mas, por acaso, não concordas com essa descrição que fiz da tua pessoa?

- Sim, ainda encabulada disse ela, devo deixar a modéstia de lado e concordar contigo, eu sei que estás me retratando fielmente e, mais uma vez, te agradeço, pela bondade e pela gentileza, muito obrigado.

- Então, minha caríssima amiga, me diga uma coisa, essas tuas lindas características físicas veem de onde?

- Não entendi, amigo, me explica melhor essa tua pergunta.

- Estas tuas lindas características, caríssima amiga, ... não são também uma ... herança genética?

Diante dessa pergunta, ela, silenciosamente, levantou-se, saiu da sala e dirigiu-se a um dos quartos do apartamento.

Quando voltou, ela, com os olhos inchados de tanto chorar, mas demonstrando querer mudar de assunto, perguntou:

- Gostastes do suco que tomamos há pouco?

- Sim, estava ótimo, aliás, foi muito boa a tua sugestão de não tomarmos vinho, pois ele teria turvado a nossa mente e isso dificultaria essa nossa conversa.

Deixando bem claro que queria encerrar a conversa, ela dirigiu-se a um pequeno refrigerador que havia na sala, pegou uma garrafa de vinho tinto, abriu-o e serviu-o em duas taças que tinha ido buscar na cristaleira.

Com a taça na mão, fizeram um brinde à saúde e começaram a tomá-lo bem lentamente e em total silêncio.

Quando terminaram de beber aquela taça, as colocaram sobre uma pequena mesa que estava em frente ao sofá e permaneceram em silêncio.

Experiência

Ele se levanta, pega o carro e sai.

No destino, ele estaciona e pega uma cadeira dobrável do porta-malas.

Lentamente, com a cadeira na mão, dirige-se ao local que a sua mente lhe havia determinado ao acordar.

Chegando, abre a cadeira, senta-se e fica olhando fixamente para aquela sepultura.

Após vários minutos, diz: pai, muito obrigado pela cinquentenária lição, tu estavas certo, eles são todos iguais.

Feminismo e acumulação de riqueza

- Oi amiga, atendendo o telefone ele a saudou.

- Oi amigo, tudo bem contigo?

- Sim, felizmente está tudo indo razoavelmente bem, mas a que devo a honra desse teu telefonema?

- Eu estava aqui meditando sobre um problema existencial que está me atormentando e eu gostaria muito de ouvir uma daquelas tuas opiniões retrógradas e duras, mas que sempre gosto de ouvir quando tenho de decidir sobre algo muito importante.

- Opa, me parece que não sou só eu que falo palavras diretas e contundentes, hein?

- Mas, falou ele demonstrando estar sorrindo, como estás com esse humor ácido, talvez esse não seja o momento adequado para conversarmos, hein?

- Tá bem, esquece, estou precisando trocar umas ideias contigo, podes vir até o meu apartamento?

- Claro, amiga, amanhã à tarde vou ao teu apartamento.

No dia seguinte, ele chegou no apartamento, tocou a campainha e quando ela abriu a porta ele entrou, deixou o calçado no vestíbulo e, seguindo a antiga rotina, se dirigiram à cozinha, pegaram copos de água e foram até a sala onde se sentaram um em cada ponta do velho sofá de três lugares.

Depois de um tempo calada, ela falou:

- Sabes, amigo, um dilema vem me atormentando há alguns anos.

Ele olhou-a indagativamente e ela continuou.

- O meu dilema, que, aliás, não é só meu, pois também vem sendo enfrentado por muitas amigas que estão na mesma faixa de idade que a minha, é sobre a maternidade.

E continuou em tom de desabafo.

- Como sabes, atualmente é muito forte o apelo para que a mulher abdique da maternidade para não ter de renunciar a muitas coisas e atividades que gostamos de realizar.

- Sim, respondeu ele, é verdade, esse é um grande dilema que as mulheres que estão chegando perto do fim do período fértil estão enfrentando e, sou testemunha de que esse fato tem deixado as mulheres muito intranquilas.

- Exatamente, respondeu ela, e é uma intranquilidade que gera um profundo estado de angústia em todas nós.

- Por acaso, perguntou ele, tens algum impedimento físico, familiar, emocional ou econômico que te impeça de procriar?

- Não, responde ela, felizmente nenhum impedimento.

- Pois então, amiga, já que não tens qualquer impedimento, nem físico, nem familiar, nem emocional e nem econômico, tens que tomar essa decisão logo, já que o teu tempo para uma gestação mais segura está quase terminando e atualmente quase não percebemos o transcorrer dos dias.

- Exatamente, concordou ela, e, se esse assunto não te incomoda, eu gostaria de dialogar contigo para conhecer quais são as nossas convergências e as nossas divergências sobre ele.

- Não, esse assunto não me incomoda, disse ele, antes pelo contrário, pois, por também não ter filhos, eu carrego dentro de mim um pouco desse teu dilema e a minha idade também me obriga a decidir logo, porque se eu decidir ter filhos tenho que tê-los ainda quando a minha idade permita que eu me comporte com eles como um pai e não como um avô.

- Sim, amigo, mas para as mulheres essa decisão tem muitas outras implicações, pois se trata de uma mudança bastante significativa tanto nos nossos corpos quanto nas nossas atividades familiares e profissionais.

- Sim, tens razão, a maternidade é bem mais complexa, mas a paternidade traz para o homem novas e importantes responsabilidades, tanto sociais quanto humanas, que alteram as suas atividades familiares e profissionais.

- Sim, concordou ela, mas a maternidade coloca a mulher frente ao desafio da tripla jornada de trabalho, pois ela, além de trabalhar, passa a ter responsabilidade de cuidar dos filhos e da casa e isso não acontece com o homem.

- Não é bem assim, amiga, o homem consciente do que significam a prole e a família também tem que mudar sensivelmente o seu comportamento tanto pessoal quanto social.

- A propósito, continuou ele, eu gostaria de muito de falar contigo sobre essa questão da tripla jornada de trabalho da mulher, pois tenho pensado muito sobre isso, e, principalmente, quando a mulher coloca essa questão sob o manto da vitimização.

- É a mais pura verdade, assentiu ela ao mesmo tempo em que adotava uma postura corporal que demonstrava forte autoconfiança.

- As mulheres são covardemente massacradas pela sociedade que ainda é muito machista, patriarcal e isso nos impele a lutar para mudar essa situação que nos é imposta pelos homens ...

- Opa, interrompeu ele, calma lá, também não é bem assim, pois há homens e homens assim como também há mulheres e mulheres.

- Olha, disse ela, eu não concordo muito com essa tua afirmativa, pois afinal, no âmago, na essência, no básico, todos os homens são iguais, são todos machistas e violentos.

- Olha, minha cara amiga, se explorarmos com profundidade essa tua afirmação talvez até tenhas um pouco de razão, já que alguns homens ameaçam utilizar, ou efetivamente utilizam, a força física para se impor perante a mulher já que ele é, em regra, fisicamente mais forte que a mulher.

- Mas, se seguirmos essa tua linha de raciocínio, continuou ele, as mulheres também seriam todas iguais, pois algumas utilizam palavras e/ou comportamentos emocionalmente destrutivos para se impor ao homem.

- A diferença, continuou ele, é que o homem, quando emprega a sua característica, que é a força física, deixa marcas físicas, portanto, marcas visíveis.

- Por sua vez, continuou, quando a mulher emprega a sua característica, que são as palavras e/ou os comportamentos, deixa marcas emocionais e psicológicas, portanto marcas não visíveis, já que ela é, em regra, psicologicamente mais forte em relação ao homem.

- E, continuou ele, as marcas emocionais e psicológicas podem ser tão ao mais difíceis de curar que as marcas físicas e, isso, seguindo a linha do teu raciocínio, coloca o homem e a mulher em condições de igualdade.

- Mas é preciso esclarecer, amiga, que entendo que nenhuma dessas duas formas de violência é exclusiva do homem ou da mulher, pois o homem também pratica violência emocional e a mulher também pratica violência física, portanto ambas precisam ser combatidas com muito vigor por todos.

Ela resolveu não retrucar e ele continuou.

- Mas, vamos encerrar essa digressão e voltar para a tal tripla jornada de trabalho que as mulheres tanto enfatizam, podes me explicar melhor essa tua opinião?

- Com certeza, a mulher, além de trabalhar, precisa cuidar dos trabalhos caseiros, cuidar da criação dos filhos, cuidar dos idosos, cuidar da segurança emocional de toda a família e cuidar da convivência com os vizinhos e com a comunidade.

- Mas, retrucou ele, essas atividades não são unicamente das mulheres, pois os homens também têm todas essas responsabilidades.

- Sim, respondeu ela, mas o homem sempre se posicionou unicamente como o provedor financeiro da família sem assumir que essas também são suas responsabilidades.

- Com isso, a mulher e a família se tornaram financeiramente dependentes do marido, que, não raro, se comporta como um ser superior que menospreza a todos e não lhes dá a mínima autonomia financeira.

- Olha, respondeu ele, esse não é o comportamento de todos os homens, portanto ao afirmares isso, estás te referindo tão somente aos homens mesquinhos, ou seja, aqueles que só se preocupam com o dinheiro e não entendem a importância da vida em família e muito menos do seu papel como ser humano.

- Esse tipo de homem, continuou ele, por ser desprezível, nunca deve ser escolhido por uma mulher, independentemente se ela tem ou não, se terá ou não, uma atividade profissional, para tê-lo como seu companheiro e muito menos para ter filhos e para constituir uma família com ele.

- As mulheres, amiga, precisam observar atentamente o caráter e a índole de um homem antes de optar por ter filhos com ele, já que um homem mesquinho nunca conseguirá sentir o genuíno júbilo de tomar uma pequenina filha nos braços e ouvi-la falar pela primeira vez a palavra *"papai"*.

- Está certo, respondeu ela, mas as mulheres também passaram a querer poder sair com as amigas, ir sozinha às festas, ter uma carreira profissional e ter independência financeira, mas o cuidado dos filhos, da casa e dos idosos lhe tira a liberdade para desfrutar dessas coisas boas da vida.

- Mas, amiga, esses cuidados de que falas também são de responsabilidade dos homens, portanto essas responsabilidades das mulheres não as impedem de ter momentos em que elas possam exercer a sua individualidade.

- Me parece, continuou ele, que estás relegando a um segundo plano algo que é muito mais importante que todas essas satisfações que mencionastes, que é a preservação da raça humana.

- Aliás, como a prerrogativa da preservação da raça coloca as mulheres em um patamar único e inatingível por qualquer homem, não me parece existir justificativa aceitável para que elas abdiquem dessa prerrogativa, desse privilégio, sem um forte motivo, um motivo que seja impeditivo da procriação.

- Muito menos, continuou ele, são inaceitáveis as justificativas de perda da liberdade, da renúncia aos prazeres mundanos, da independência financeira e das conquistas profissionais.

À medida que ele falava, ela ia se enrodilhando no sofá.

- Aliás, continuou ele, nós precisamos examinar melhor essa questão da independência financeira e das conquistas profissionais, pois eu acredito que esses temas tenham ganhado grande impulso nos debates também por interesse de grupos que objetivavam ganhos econômicos e financeiros.

- Opa, agora eu é que digo, calma lá amigo, e endireitando o corpo e posicionando os pés firmemente no chão, falou:

- A independência financeira e as conquistas profissionais são duas grandes conquistas das mulheres que antes viviam dependentes dos maridos o que, felizmente, hoje já está bastante mitigado.

- Sim, tens razão amiga, a mulher passou a ter rendimentos com trabalhos fora de casa e esse é o ponto que eu gostaria de aprofundar mais, pois me parece que está faltando uma análise mais ampla sobre todo esse belo movimento igualitarista entre o homem e a mulher bravamente promovido pelas mulheres e por muitos homens.

- Sem a menor dúvida, continuou ele, esse movimento gerou essas conquistas, mas que, no caso de algumas mulheres, e esse é o meu ponto de discordância, essas conquistas foram atingidas em detrimento da maternidade e da abdicação do grande papel exercido pelas mulheres no âmbito familiar.

- E tenho cá minhas dúvidas, continuou ele, sobre se esse excelente movimento igualitarista não tenha sido manipulado por pessoas que defenderam a inclusão da mulher no mercado de trabalho, principalmente na idade em que ela tem mais capacidade produtiva, para obter benefícios econômicos e financeiros e, com isso, concentrar renda e poder.

- Aliás, continuou ele, chegamos a ler textos e a ouvir discursos que menosprezavam a maternidade e que sugeriam que as mulheres não deveriam optar por ela para não retardar o início das suas jornadas profissionais.

Nesse momento, ela o interrompeu e perguntou:

- Podes me explicar melhor esse teu ponto de vista sobre a manipulação econômica e financeira do movimento feminista?

- Veja, disse ele, somente para fins de explicitar melhor esse meu ponto de vista, vamos tomar como hipótese a existência de um país que tenha uma população economicamente ativa dividida em metade homens e metade mulheres.

- E que nesse nosso hipotético exemplo a massa trabalhadora disponível para o mercado seja formada pelos homens e que as mulheres permaneçam em casa.

- Vamos admitir também que em um pequeno período essas mulheres que estão em casa passem a ter uma carreira profissional e, na sequência, passem a buscar um trabalho fora de casa.

- Ao também passarem a participar da massa trabalhadora disponível para o mercado, elas duplicariam a oferta de mão de obra e gerariam um imediato e grande desequilíbrio entre a oferta e a procura de mão de obra.

- Essa hipótese nos leva a duas perguntas:

- Quem se beneficiaria com essa duplicação da oferta da mão de obra?

- O que aconteceria com economia desse país?

- Não é difícil concluir que os empregadores passariam a se aproveitar dessa mudança de paradigma social para pagar menores salários para as mulheres e para reduzir a quantidade de homens empregados.

- Com a consolidação dessa situação, os empregadores passariam a ter os seus custos com mão de obra profundamente reduzidos, e, consequentemente, passariam a ter maiores lucros.

- Além disso, o ingresso massivo das mulheres no mercado de trabalho provocaria uma considerável ampliação do mercado de consumo, pois haveria um grande aumento da demanda por bens e serviços.

- As mulheres passariam a ter necessidade de adquirir, por exemplo, mais roupas, mais calçados e mais produtos para o cabelo e para o corpo.

Elas também demandariam meios de transporte, como motos e automóveis, e equipamentos para a automatização dos serviços caseiros.

- Todo esse movimento econômico provocaria um sensível aumento dos preços dos bens e serviços e uma sensível queda dos salários que viria a se somar a já existente queda em decorrência da substituição da mão de obra por máquinas.

- Nesse nosso exemplo, os grandes beneficiados dessa repentina duplicação de mão de obra disponível seriam os empregadores, as empresas fabricantes e vendedoras de mercadorias, as empresas prestadoras de serviços e, claro, o governo, já que este passaria a arrecadar mais impostos com o incremento da atividade econômica.

- A propósito, já li e ouvi pessoas defendendo o movimento feminista como sendo uma grande e imperdível oportunidade de negócios para o mercado.

- Com isso, a crise da renda do trabalhador se aprofundaria por gerar uma forte concorrência pela renda assalariada disponível, que provocaria um aumento do ambiente de conflito social, inclusive, entre os casais.

- Esses movimentos econômicos provocariam uma forte aceleração do processo de concentração da renda nas mãos das poucas pessoas que detém o poder sobre os empregos e sobre a produção de bens e serviços.

- Pois bem, minha amiga, voltando para a nossa realidade, foi exatamente isso que aconteceu em nosso país e em boa parte do mundo, só que, como essa mudança foi ocorrendo ao longo das últimas décadas, o impacto econômico também foi sendo gradativamente sentido.

- Eu acredito, continuou ele, que essa mudança tenha contribuído para o aumento e a consolidação das chamadas riquezas dinásticas, que concentram a renda mundial nas mãos de poucas famílias e que levou imensas massas de trabalhadores a viver na miséria ou em situação de mera subsistência.

Nesse momento, ela o interrompeu e disse:

- Mas a mulher sempre foi muito desprestigiada, pois os trabalhos caseiros, a criação dos filhos, o cuidado dos idosos, a segurança emocional de toda a família e a convivência com os vizinhos e com a comunidade não estavam sendo reconhecidos.

- Como essas atividades não eram valorizadas nem pela sociedade nem pelos homens, as mulheres passaram a rejeitá-las e a buscar um espaço no mercado de trabalho, continuou ela.

- Tens razão, respondeu ele, mas me parece que em resposta a essa falta de prestígio o movimento igualitarista não lutou pelo retorno da antiga valorização e optou a ser um mero movimento de promoção de disputas para ocupação do mercado de trabalho.

- E para justificar a defesa da mudança do paradigma social as mulheres passaram a desprestigiar e a rejeitar o importante papel que estavam desempenhando na sociedade e, dessa forma, se tornaram cúmplices dos que se beneficiaram da mudança.

- Ao abandonar esses papeis absolutamente essenciais e muito superiores a qualquer salário ou a qualquer renda, elas permitiram que esses papeis fossem terceirizados, inclusive para empresas como as de serviços domésticos, creches e escolas.

- E entre esses papéis que foram transferidos foi transferido o maior de todos que é o de educar e dar equilíbrio emocional à família e em especial à prole.

- A propósito, fala-se muito que a violência contra a mulher decorre de falta de educação, mas justamente esse importantíssimo papel social, o da educação e o do equilíbrio emocional da prole, foi desprestigiado pelo próprio movimento feminista.

- E esse contexto prejudicou fortemente a educação das crianças, que é justamente o que promove e sustenta valores que visam uma sociedade mais sadia e mais humana.

- A propósito, é importante registrar que a sistêmica familiar se reflete fortemente no comportamento das pessoas e por conseguinte se refletirá nas futuras famílias, no tipo de gestão que será adotada pelos administradores das empresas privadas e no tipo de gestão que será adotada pelos governantes das coisas públicas, que têm influência decisiva nos rumos de qualquer sociedade.

- Além disso, continuou ele, o movimento feminista, ao passar a lutar por prestígio e por espaço no mercado de trabalho e não pelo reconhecimento e pela valorização das atividades que as mulheres desempenhavam e ao se aliar ao dito mercado, ele incentivou a mulher a deixar de se dedicar a todo conjunto familiar para se dedicar mais profundamente na obtenção de conquistas profissionais e financeiras.

- A propósito, continuou ele, as próprias mulheres chegaram a carimbar essas importantes atividades que desempenhavam como atividades degradantes, que, frisa-se, se essas atividades fossem adequadamente valoradas elas superariam em muito os valores gerados por muitas outras atividades econômicas.

- O absurdo, continuou ele, ficou mais evidente ainda quando elas passaram a deixar de lado essas atividades imensamente superiores para se submeterem a trabalhar em ambientes prejudiciais à saúde e emocionalmente tóxicos.

- Em empregos que transformam as pessoas em meros robôs, que submetem os trabalhadores a tarefas de movimentos repetitivos, que exigem exagerada produtividade, que são exercidos em locais insalubres e que monitoram os trabalhadores até quando se afastam do local de trabalho para irem ao banheiro ou ao bebedouro de água.

Nesse momento ela o interrompe diz:

- Mas as mulheres aceitaram essas condições humilhantes de trabalho para se verem livres da dominação do homem por ser ele o único membro que obtinha a renda necessária para a sobrevivência do núcleo familiar.

- E assim, continuou ela, passou a existir dentro da família uma forte hierarquia com o homem ocupando a posição mais elevada e que, por isso, era chamado, inclusive oficialmente, por "chefe de família".

- Sim, tens razão, disse ele, havia quem defendesse a ideia, que também era governamentalmente reforçada, de que o sistema familiar deveria ser baseado na dominação do homem por meio da chamada hierarquia de gênero.

- Mas isso não pode ser encarado como uma realidade monolítica, pois no núcleo familiar nem sempre havia e não pode haver qualquer tipo de hierarquia e muito menos uma hierarquia baseada na renda, posto que essa, definitivamente, não é a mais importante nem para a família nem para a sociedade.

- No entanto, continuou ele, aqui nos defrontamos com o grande paradoxo do movimento feminista, que buscou abrir espaço justamente no mercado de trabalho onde a hierarquia é uma regra absoluta.

- Ou seja, o movimento lutou para tirar a mulher de uma nem sempre existente hierarquia familiar para integrá-la ao mercado de trabalho que funciona sempre sob uma permanente e dura hierarquia empresarial.

E continuou ele em tom de forte convicção.

- O movimento feminista ao defender as ideias de que o trabalho não remunerado do ambiente familiar não era importante, de que no ambiente familiar existia a hierarquia baseada no gênero masculino e de que a renda era a definidora dessa hierarquia, o movimento feminista foi ao encontro dos interesses dos concentradores de riqueza, ou seja, o movimento feminista empurrou as mulheres para um ambiente dominador por excelência.

- Para atingir esse objetivo, o movimento feminista acabou optando pela depreciação do papel da mulher na família e pela realização de uma aliança tácita com o dito mercado que estava em busca de uma maior oferta de mão de obra e de uma ampliação do mercado de consumo.

- Assim, o mercado atraiu para o seu lado um movimento que abandonou a importante luta pela ampla igualdade entre a mulher e o homem para focar somente na igualdade de renda.

Ele fez uma pequena pausa e continuou.

- Abordando essa opção a partir de um ponto de observação mais distante, vemos que, ao defender somente a questão financeira pessoal, o movimento feminista acabou replicando a prática atual da financeirização dos mercados, que não se preocupa com a sociedade onde as suas empresas estão instaladas tão pouco se preocupa com a saúde negocial das próprias empresas, mas tão somente com o lucro financeiro imediato que pode ser obtido.

- Um exemplo claro dessa financeirização dos mercados são os grandes conglomerados empresariais que são formados a partir da aquisição de várias empresas por grupos financeiros que visam a máxima dominação possível do mercado em que atuam para gerar altos retornos financeiros.

- Sem a menor dúvida, é um grande contrassenso o movimento feminista, que luta incansavelmente contra um dito processo de dominação familiar, lutar para participar do dito mercado que está cada vez mais concentrado e, consequentemente, mais dominador.

Nesse momento ela o replica:

- Mas o movimento feminista foi muito além desta questão financeira e profissional, pois ao longo do tempo ele provocou um produtivo debate sobre a igualdade entre homens e mulheres, sobre a erradicação do machismo patriarcal, sobre o direito ao voto, sobre a igualdade de gênero, sobre o direito de propriedade, sobre o direito de contratar, sobre o fim do etnocentrismo, sobre o direito à sexualidade, sobre o isolamento social feminino, e por aí vai, meu amigo.

- Opa, amiga, tens toda a razão, e é por isso, pela amplitude desse movimento social, que eu prefiro chamá-lo de movimento igualitarista, já que considero a palavra feminista como redutora da importância dele.

- E digo mais, continuou ele, esse movimento igualitarista foi extremamente importante para a evolução da sociedade humana, mas, que, infelizmente, em muitas vezes esses importantes assuntos que citastes foram deixados de lado para priorizar o debate sobre o tema das conquistas profissionais e da independência financeira.

- Mas, cara amiga, vamos deixar claro que a minha fala está centrada na opção pela independência financeira em detrimento da maternidade e não contra o movimento igualitarista das mulheres.

- A minha grande dúvida é se a priorização do debate sobre as conquistas profissionais e sobre a independência financeira das mulheres não foi fortemente impulsionada por aqueles que ganharam muito com essa movimentação econômica, ou seja, se esse movimento não foi, de certo modo, manipulado por aqueles que queriam acumular riqueza e, consequentemente, mais poder.

- A propósito, essa manipulação pode ser observada em textos amplamente divulgados, inclusive em fóruns mundiais, que estimam que, no atual ritmo, serão necessários mais de 150 anos para que as disparidades salariais entre os homens e as mulheres sejam corrigidas.

- Além disso, continuou ele, a captura do movimento feminista também pode ser constatada em textos e falas que defendem a igualdade entre homens e mulheres, mas por ser essa igualdade importante para o dito fortalecimento da economia e não por ser importante para o fortalecimento da mulher e da sociedade humana.

- Aliás, nada pode estar mais a favor dos acumuladores de renda do que as manifestações que consideram a menopausa como um sério problema econômico por causar a queda da produtividade da mulher bem como as manifestações que consideram a maternidade como uma penalidade que é imposta às mulheres.

- Mas, amiga, vamos deixar bem claro que não estou falando que as mulheres não devam ter seus próprios rendimentos, pois, voltando ao início da nossa conversa, estamos falando sobre a mulher que, para desfrutar de prazeres mundanos e para ter conquistas profissionais e independência financeira, abdica da prerrogativa exclusiva que a coloca em um patamar único e inatingível por qualquer homem, que é o da preservação da raça humana.

- Mas, calma lá, disse ela, o homem também tem responsabilidade pela preservação da raça.

- Sim, com certeza amiga, mas o homem é facilmente substituível enquanto a mulher não, ela é insubstituível.

- Mas, disse ela, há homem que também deixa de procriar para priorizar os prazeres mundanos e o sucesso profissional, que, aliás, me parece ser o teu caso, afinal tu também não tens filhos.

- Sim, tens toda razão amiga, e, por isso, me penitencio todos os dias e por isso é que estou gostando tanto de falar contigo sobre esse assunto, pois essa conversa me permite desabafar com essa mulher que eu tanto respeito e admiro.

- Aliás, continuou ele, tanto a responsabilidade é dos dois que talvez até seja por isso que no nosso idioma as palavras maternidade e paternidade tenham o mesmo número de letras e apenas se diferenciam pela letra inicial, ou seja uma diferença muito tênue entre elas.

- Mas, a propósito, um detalhe que me chama muito a atenção, continuou ele, é que muitas pessoas defendem a inclusão da mulher no mercado do trabalho em detrimento da maternidade afirmando que isso proporciona uma maior equidade nas atividades caseiras entre o homem e a mulher.

- No entanto, essas mesmas pessoas, que, de certa forma, constrangem as mulheres a fazerem a opção pela carreira profissional, não fazem nenhum esforço para também constranger os homens a assumirem os nobres papéis caseiros.

- Ou seja, o mesmo esforço que é feito para incentivar as mulheres a ingressarem no mercado de trabalho também deveria ser feito para que o homem machista patriarcal se desarraigue dessas práticas e atitudes antissociais.

- E aí também vejo aquela possível manipulação do movimento de que falei antes, pois essa omissão intencional beneficia fortemente os empregadores.

- Mas, continuou ele, voltando ao meu caso pessoal, hoje tenho plena consciência desse meu comportamento e, como não tenho qualquer impedimento, estou querendo mudar a minha vida, estou querendo ter filhos, estou querendo constituir uma família, estou querendo assumir esses nobres papeis caseiros.

- Nada, absolutamente nada, continuou ele, é comparável a gerar, criar e educar uma criança, que, aliás, foi graças a decisão a favor da procriação, independentemente de terem tido ou não uma atividade profissional, tomadas pelas nossas mães e pelos nossos pais é que podemos estar aqui tendo essa agradável conversa.

- E tem mais, ...

Nesse momento, ela deu um pulo do sofá, colocou-se em pé e com voz forte e determinada disse:

- Ok, amigo, podemos parar por aqui mesmo, para mim está bom assim, te proponho parar de falar sobre esse assunto.

E, conseguindo interromper a fala dele, ela imediatamente dirigiu-se a um pequeno refrigerador que havia na sala tirou de dentro dele uma garrafa de vinho tinto e perguntou:

- Vamos tomar uma taça desse vinho?

- Ganhei esse vinho de uma amiga e eu gosto muito dele porque durante o processo de produção não foram adicionados sulfitos, dessa maneira ele contém somente aqueles que são gerados naturalmente durante o processo da própria vinificação.

E continuou falando daquele assunto que ela dominava como poucas pessoas.

- Ele não me dá dor de cabeça e nem dor de estômago, que são os sintomas que por vezes sinto quando ao vinho foi adicionado excesso de sulfito, como é chamado o anidrido sulforoso, que é adicionado aos vinhos para fins de conservação.

- Ok, muito bom, não precisa dar mais detalhes, já me convencestes, eu aceito a oferta, podes trazer a garrafa e as taças, disse ele.

Ela buscou duas taças na cristaleira e serviu o vinho, que estava na temperatura ideal para ser consumido, até ocupar três quartos do volume da taça, fizeram um brinde à saúde e começaram a tomá-lo lenta e silenciosamente.

Quando terminaram de beber, colocaram as taças sobre uma pequena mesa que ficava em frente ao sofá e permaneceram em silêncio.

Após a transcurso de um bom tempo, ela deslizou lentamente a mão para o meio do sofá indicando que gostaria de pegar a mão dele e ele, correspondendo ao gesto dela, também estendeu a mão e pegou delicadamente a mão dela.

Neste momento, de mãos dadas, ela falou:

- Sabes, esse nosso encontro foi ótimo, pois eu me encontrei comigo mesma.

- Eu também, respondeu ele, e te agradeço o convite para essa proveitosa conversa, pois eu também me encontrei comigo mesmo.

Após uma breve pausa, ela perguntou:

- Ficas comigo esta noite?

E ele, prontamente, respondeu:

- Com certeza, fico, e com ampla, total e irrestrita disposição.

Assim, cada um sentado no seu canto do sofá, mas com as mãos fortemente entrelaçadas, adormeceram.

Simbiose perfeita

Ele estava arrasado.

A grande aflição que o assolava há vários meses havia começado quando uma sequência de péssimos acontecimentos começaram a ocorrer na sua vida.

Ele tinha a impressão de que o mundo havia caído sobre a sua cabeça.

Tudo começou quando num dia ele acordou e encontrou o seu gato de estimação morto sobre o tapete.

Como o gato tinha vinte anos, ele sabia que isso estava prestes a ocorrer, mas, mesmo assim, ele foi tomado por uma enorme tristeza.

Poucos dias após a namorada pela qual ele era apaixonado lhe mandou uma mensagem dizendo que o queria muito bem, mas que entendia que a relação deles deveria ser encerrada, já que ela pretendia dar outro rumo para a vida dela.

Naquele mesmo dia, ele havia recebido um aviso que uma das casas de veraneio que ele tinha em um balneário havia sido invadida pelas águas da intensa chuva que havia caído naquela região.

Esta sequência de fatos o deixou tão abatido que chegou a pensar em suicídio, mas chegou à conclusão de que ele não teria coragem para praticar esse ato extremo.

Mas a angústia, a desolação, a aflição que lhe envolvia era tão intensa que ele sentia que precisava se envolver com algo que o tirasse daquela situação e resolveu viajar em busca de um lenitivo.

Comprou uma passagem e foi para um país distante e por ele desconhecido.

Quando chegou ao destino, alugou um carro e saiu sem rumo.

Entrava em uma estrada, mudava repentinamente para outra e quando estava chegando a noite ele parava no primeiro hotel ou na primeira pousada que aparecia em seu caminho.

Num dia, como não encontrou lugar para se hospedar, ele dirigiu até cansar e parou no acostamento de uma estrada vicinal onde pegou no sono sentado no banco do carro.

Ele dormiu de uma maneira muito desconfortável, mas, pensou, tudo aquilo era melhor que estar em casa e ter de enfrentar todos aqueles acontecimentos que ainda continuavam lhe atormentando.

A vontade do suicídio não lhe saia da cabeça e por mais de uma vez ele pensou em atirar o carro contra um daqueles enormes caminhões com que cruzava na estrada, mas quando teve a oportunidade de assim proceder acabou recuando por lhe faltar a necessária coragem.

Em uma manhã, após sair de um pequeno e sujo quarto que ele havia alugado em um posto de gasolina para passar a noite, ele parou ao pé uma enorme montanha.

Olhou para o mapa eletrônico instalado no carro e viu que havia uma pequena estrada sem pavimento que subia pela encosta até o cume.

Constatou na internet que aquela montanha era um vulcão que ainda estava ativo e que apresentava sinais de atividade com tímidas colunas de fumaça que saiam da cratera e eventualmente do respiradouro, portanto a possibilidade de uma repentina erupção era tão concreta quanto imprevisível.

Pensou, repensou e resolveu seguir por aquela estrada que o levaria ao cume.

Começou a subida e verificou que ele precisaria dirigir com muita atenção, pois, além de íngreme e sem pavimento, a estrada estava repleta de pedras soltas que o obrigava a progredir muito lentamente.

Enquanto subia, pensava que se algo de ruim lhe acontecesse naquele vulcão ele aceitaria bem, pois a aflição que as perdas que ele havia tido, o gato, a namorada e a casa, não lhe deixavam a mente.

Quando estava próximo da cratera, ele viu que uma parte da encosta havia sido aplainada nela haviam sido construídos um amplo estacionamento e uma casa de dois pisos.

Estacionou o carro e verificou que a casa tinha no piso térreo uma loja típica de locais turísticos, que vendia alimentos, bebidas não alcoólicas, objetos e utensílios para longas caminhadas e uma infinidade de produtos artesanais que eram vendidos como lembrança daquele lugar.

Verificou também que o piso superior da casa era uma residência, que com certeza, dada a distância da cidade mais próxima, seria a moradia das pessoas que ali trabalhavam.

Desceu do carro e nem se preocupou em fechá-lo, pois o dele era o único no estacionamento, e dirigiu-se, lentamente, para a loja.

Entrou e uma senhora de cabelos brancos o recebeu com um largo sorriso de boas-vindas.

- Bom dia, senhor. – disse a simpática senhora.

- Bom dia, a senhora pode me servir uma água e um sanduíche? – perguntou ele.

- Com certeza, e com o maior prazer, senhor.

Ele se sentou à mesa e aguardou.

A senhora logo chegou com a água e o sanduíche e ele puxou uma conversa com ela.

- A senhora trabalha aqui?

- Sim, eu trabalho e moro aqui, este é o canto do mundo que escolhi para viver.

Mas há outras pessoas, outros funcionários que lhe ajudam?

- Não, não há mais ninguém, o meu marido faleceu, os meus filhos foram estudar e trabalhar na cidade e eu decidi continuar aqui morando e trabalhando sozinha.

- Mas é um lugar bem ermo, a senhora não se sente solitária?

- Não, absolutamente, eu sempre tenho a companhia dos turistas e do meu trabalho e quando a noite chega vou dormir satisfeita e tranquila.

- A senhora está aqui há muitos anos?

- Sim, estou aqui desde jovem quando me casei e junto com meu marido montamos essa loja e construímos a nossa residência.

- Aqui tive meus filhos, meus animais de estimação e uma vida excelente com o meu falecido marido.

- Onde estão os seus animais de estimação?

- Todos eles morreram. – respondeu ela.

- A senhora vive bem próximo da cratera do vulcão que ainda está em atividade e isso não lhe dá medo? não lhe deixa aflita, desolada?

- Não, de jeito nenhum, eu vivo bem tranquila e não penso em sair daqui, pois aqui é o meu canto do mundo onde tive os melhores momentos da minha vida.

- Mas se o vulcão entrar em erupção a senhora vai ficar e correr o risco de morrer?

- Nada disso, se a erupção vier eu saio daqui imediatamente, pois eu gosto muito da minha vida e não pretendo me suicidar.

- Mas com uma eventual erupção a senhora perderá tudo, já perdeu o marido, os filhos, os animais de estimação e perderá também esse patrimônio.

- Sim, eu sei disso.

- Mas esse vulcão me deu tudo o que eu tenho, portanto ele pode me tomar essa parte do meu patrimônio quando ele quiser.

- Veja, caro senhor, essa casa é apenas uma pequena parte do meu patrimônio, pois a vida que ele me proporcionou e os filhos que eu criei aqui ele não me exigirá de volta, então eu não posso me queixar se ele resolver me tomar esse bem material.

A objetividade do raciocínio daquela senhora, a associação, a interação, a simbiose que ela tinha com aquela montanha e com a natureza, o deixou mudo e envergonhado de si mesmo.

Com lágrimas correndo em suas faces e meneando a cabeça para concordar com ela, ele se levantou, pagou a conta, lhe deu um forte aperto de mão e um consentido e longo abraço e disse-lhe: muito, muito, muito obrigado, caríssima senhora.

Ele voltou imediatamente para a sua casa e recomeçou a viver com essa lição que ele nunca mais esqueceu.

Residência

Chorando, ele inicia o trajeto de volta à casa onde a esposa o esperava com, como sempre fazia, o jantar à mesa.

Próximo de chegar em casa ele se conteve, parou de chorar e enxugou os olhos e as faces.

Sentaram-se à mesa e começaram a comer e a conversar sobre o dia de cada um deles e ela percebeu que os olhos dele estavam inchados e vermelhos.

Após os primeiros diálogos, ela fala:

- Tu não estás me contando tudo sobre o teu dia.

- Como sabes? - perguntou ele.

- Os teus olhos estão vermelhos e inchados, tu chorastes?

- Sim - disse ele, contendo os soluços.

- Hoje estou destroçado, o mundo desabou sobre a minha cabeça e estou me sentindo o mais pobre dos homens.

- Ei, meu amor, calma lá, afinal estamos com excelente saúde e isso é uma enorme riqueza.

- Mas, afinal, o que aconteceu?

- Fui demitido.

- Estou desempregado!

- Puxa, que notícia ruim - disse ela.

- Sim, muito ruim.

- A partir de hoje já não tenho uma renda garantida e na minha idade será muito difícil conseguir outro emprego, pois os empregadores têm dado preferência para trabalhadores mais jovens.

- Mas tens enorme experiência, com certeza isso vai ajudar bastante a conseguires um novo trabalho - disse ela.

- Infelizmente é justamente a experiência que vai me atrapalhar para obter uma nova colocação.

- Como assim, me explica melhor isso.

- A empresa foi comprada por um grupo financeiro que vem adquirindo várias empresas do mesmo setor para integrá-las a fim de reduzir custos e, com isso, gerar altos retornos financeiros para os gestores e para os investidores.

- Eles não se preocupam em ganhar com as operações tradicionais das empresas integradas, mas sim somente com o fluxo de caixa imediato.

- E isso eles vão conseguindo reduzindo custos e atrasando pagamentos e, consequentemente, esgarçando a relação com os funcionários, com os fornecedores e com todos os que negociam com eles.

- Com esse foco na redução de custos, normalmente, eles começam com a integração dos setores de logística das empresas adquiridas para poder reduzir o número de funcionários, de veículos, de depósitos e de rotas de entrega.

E continuou, cada vez mais triste.

- E foi o que aconteceu na minha empresa, que teve o departamento de logística, onde eu trabalhava, integrado com os de outras empresas que passaram a fazer parte de um único grupo.

- Esse processo de contínuas reduções de custo é tão intenso que os funcionários que subsistem ao processo inicial de integração logo são substituídos por outros mais jovens, pois os novos gestores aplicam um método administrativo que tem como objetivo central a alta rotatividade dos funcionários.

- É um modelo de gestão imediatista, no qual os gestores buscam rápidos e fartos resultados financeiros para distribuir altos dividendos e, com isso, adquirirem a simpatia dos acionistas para serem recompensados com altíssimas remunerações e benefícios de toda ordem.

- Sim, mas como os mais jovens entram nessa história? - perguntou ela.

- A ideia é bem simples. – disse ele.

- Como os jovens recém-formados necessitam ingressar no mercado de trabalho, eles chegam com baixa expectativa financeira e são mais maleáveis e moldáveis por não serem influenciados pela experiência.

- Não entendi isso que falastes sobre a influência da experiência - disse ela.

- Pois é, os funcionários mais antigos normalmente se preocupam com os destinos da empresa e tendem a questionar uma ou outra ordem que possa vir a prejudicar a empresa a médio ou a longo prazo e esse comportamento incomoda os gestores porque pode atrapalhar o atingimento das metas de alta e rápida geração de caixa que eles buscam.

- Como os jovens não têm essa experiência, eles tendem a ser menos seletivos e cumprem, com toda a energia que a juventude lhes proporciona, qualquer ordem que lhes é dada, pois esses gestores trabalham na base do comando rígido, na base do manda quem pode e obedece quem precisa.

- E esse processo de alta rotatividade acaba também atingindo os diretores quando eles não conseguem mais apresentar altos resultados positivos, que, muitas vezes, foi conseguido graças a artifícios, manipulações e fraudes contábeis de toda ordem, que produzem falsos lucros.

- Até os governos são envolvidos por essa falsa modalidade de administração, que é vendida como moderna e decorrente do espírito animal do investidor e que, geralmente, acaba na falência das empresas.

- E, quando isso acontece, os investidores procuram transferir para os governos o problema do desemprego em massa enquanto se deslocam para outros setores aplicando sempre a mesma técnica.

- Bem, mas com a tua experiência podemos sobreviver fazendo algumas atividades alternativas - disse ela.

- Sim, com certeza,, mas corremos o risco de sermos incluídos na população dos "sem-sem": sem-renda, sem-consumo, sem-escola, sem-hospital, sem-voz, sem-teto, ou seja, pessoas sem-cidadania e sem-dignidade.

- Nós vamos dar um jeito - disse ela.

Mas e se perdermos a nossa casa e virarmos mais um casal sem-teto? vamos morar embaixo da ponte? virias comigo?

- Com toda a certeza, meu amor, contigo eu vou morar embaixo da ponte onde teremos a nossa nova residência e posso te assegurar que no entorno da nossa casinha eu plantarei muitas flores para que ela fique sempre muito bonita.

Assim, com a parceria renovada, eles foram dormir e esperar o dia seguinte para continuar construindo o caminho que continuariam percorrendo juntos.

Guerra aos pijamas

Pijamas?
Não!

Esses indesejados,
esses inconvenientes,
precisamos transformá-los em pano de chão,
precisamos incinerá-los,
precisamos transformá-los em cinzas.

Pijamas?
Não!

Eles perturbam a sintonia fina,
eles bloqueiam o contato das peles,
eles barram o encontro das carnes,
eles atrapalham a troca dos suores.

Pijamas?
Não!

Eles impedem a fantástica sinfonia carnal,
eles obstruem o divino concerto das almas,
eles inviabilizam a simbiose perfeita.

Pijamas?
Não!

Esses indesejados,
esses inconvenientes,
precisamos transformá-los em pano de chão,
precisamos incinerá-los,
precisamos transformá-los em cinzas.

Aeroporto

A tua cama é o meu maisquerido, o meu insubstituível aeroporto.

O meu passaporte é a tua sugestiva e amorosa permissão.

Com ele e a partir dele, eu parto para as viagens mais enriquecedoras, deslumbrantes e prazerosas que alguém possa fazer no planeta terra.

Ao olhar os teus olhos sinto estar diante de dois lagos de águas de cor azul celestial que são alimentados pelo derretimento das geleiras próximas aos polos e que me proporcionam uma incomparável paz interior.

Ao passear as minhas mãos pelas tuas faces tenho o mesmo prazer de quando estou diante daqueles anjos lindíssimos representados nas pinturas e esculturas expostas nos principais museus e templos religiosos do mundo.

Ao tocar os teus lábios com os meus dedos sinto a mesma euforia de quando estou parado diante da cratera principal de um grande, majestoso e misterioso vulcão transformada em um enorme e deslumbrante lago, mas que, a qualquer momento, pode entrar em erupção transformando rochas em lavas incandescentes e tendo o poder de formar novas paisagens e novos e fecundos solos.

Ao percorrer os teus seios com as minhas mãos experimento a mesma emoção de montanhista ao escalar as mais pitorescas, desafiadoras e icônicas montanhas da terra.

Ao apalpar as tuas mãos sou envolvido pela mesma beleza de quando passeio pelas ilhas construídas dentro de plácidos mares.

Ao percorrer o teu abdômen sinto-me andando a pé e perfeitamente integrado na mais bela planície do planeta terra onde o vento core livre, leve e solto.

Ao passar as minhas pernas nas tuas sinto-me percorrendo os tubos aceleradores de partículas existentes nos principais centros de pesquisa do mundo, que permitem acelerar e chocar partículas atômicas que buscam compreender o comportamento mais íntimo da matéria.

Ao mover os meus pés nos teus me vejo diante daquelas placas que indicam direções que orienta os passantes nos pontos mais desabitados pontos do mundo.

Definitivamente, durante o tempo em que aceitares o meu passaporte, a tua cama será o meu indeclinável e insubstituível aeroporto.

Emoções

Eles estavam radiantes; a felicidade era tanta que não cabiam dentro de si a ponto de sentirem uma sensação de que iam explodir de tanta alegria.

Formavam um casal de jovens recém-casados com a mesma história de muitos outros: se encontraram, namoraram por longo tempo, conversaram muito, trocaram opiniões sobre os mais variados assuntos e chegaram à conclusão de que ambos pensavam em se casar, em ter filhos, em constituir uma família tradicional e em ter uma casa com jardim onde poderiam plantar flores e caminhar com os pés descalços na grama juntamente com filhos e animais de estimação.

Como haviam conversado muito, sabiam das dificuldades que certamente haveriam de enfrentar nesse caminho que se propunham a abrir juntos, mas, mesmo assim, após vários anos amadurecendo excepcionalmente bem a ideia com muito diálogo e assunção de compromissos mútuos, eles decidiram constituir uma família e celebraram o tão debatido casamento.

Alugaram um imóvel para morar enquanto procuravam um outro que se adaptasse ao principal plano deles que era o de ter filhos.

Naquela noite, ao receberam a confirmação de que ela estava grávida eles ficaram radiantes.

- Meu amor, disse ela, vamos marcar umas férias e fazer um passeio para celebrarmos esse momento tão especial para nós dois?

- Com certeza, respondeu ele, amanhã cedo vamos nos programar e sair.

Tudo ajustado, chegou o tão esperado dia de sair para comemorar a gravidez, que já estava aparente.

Ela havia comprado um belo vestido de grávida feito com um tecido estampado com lindas flores rosas e azuis, que despertava a atenção das pessoas pela jovialidade tanto do tecido quanto da confecção, pois ela queria compartilhar com todos a imensa felicidade que a envolvia.

Ele também havia comprado um bonito conjunto de calça, camisa e jaqueta com cores que formavam um belíssimo dégradé, que iam de um azul mais escuro para um azul celestial.

Felizes, pegaram o automóvel e partiram com destino a uma bela cidade turística que ficava há algumas dezenas de quilômetros da moradia deles.

Após duas horas de viagem rodando sempre abaixo do limite de velocidade da rodovia para melhor aproveitar o passeio e para não se colocarem em risco, eles decidiram parar em um pequeno restaurante à beira da estrada para um breve descanso, fazer um lanche e irem ao banheiro.

Ele estacionou no pátio do restaurante o automóvel que haviam anteriormente adquirido já pensando no aumento da família, que tinha espaço para colocar a cadeira de bebê, o berço, a mala com o enxoval e a sacola com todos os produtos necessários para proporcionar conforto para o futuro filho.

Calmamente, desceram do automóvel, respiraram o ar puro que havia naquele ponto ermo da rodovia e entraram no salão do restaurante onde estavam três homens sentados em uma mesa e um outro homem que estava em pé e com os braços apoiados sobre o balcão de atendimento dos clientes.

Alegres e sorridentes, cumprimentaram os três homens sentados e, em seguida, cumprimentaram o homem do balcão, que demonstrava ser o dono do restaurante, e perguntaram-lhe se poderiam utilizar os sanitários o que foi respondido com um leve, positivo e sério balançar de cabeça.

A alegria e a descontração era tanta que não notaram que nenhum dos quatro homens havia retribuído aos cordiais cumprimento deles.

Quando voltaram dos sanitários, pediram dois sanduíches e duas garrafas de água e sentaram-se em uma mesa onde ficaram conversando alegremente esperando que o homem do balcão, que estava preparando os sanduíches, os avisasse estavam prontos.

Quando receberam o aviso de que estavam prontos, eles foram buscar e começaram a comer e continuaram conversando alegremente.

Ao, despretensiosamente, olharem ao redor verificaram que todos os quatro homens os observavam fixamente, mas não levaram isso em conta e continuaram comendo e conversando tranquilamente.

Todos os quatro homens tinham um aspecto de serem pessoas que haviam passado muito trabalho, pois tinham características rudes e semblantes bem tensos.

Cada um dos que estavam sentados à mesa tinham uma característica que chamava atenção: um usava um espesso bigode, outro tinha um corte em uma das orelhas e o outro usava sapatos com solados de tamanhos diferentes o que indicava que ele tinha uma perna mais curta do que a outra.

De repente, o que tinha um corte na orelha levantou-se, caminhou de maneira trôpega em direção à mesa dos dois e, com a voz lenta e pastosa que demonstrava os efeitos de bebida alcoólica, falou:

- Você é muito bonita, dirigindo-se à jovem esposa.

O jovem esposo, meio sem jeito, antecipou-se e respondeu respeitosamente:

- Muito obrigado, eu fico contente com o elogio que o senhor dirigiu a minha esposa.

Ela, desconfortada, agradeceu o elogio com um protocolar sorriso, mas amarelo, nos lábios.

O homem deu mais um passo em direção à jovem esposa e, chegando ao lado dela, passou uma das suas mãos nos braços dela e disse:

- Você tem uma pele tão macia que me dá vontade de tocar.

No mesmo instante em que a jovem esposa recolhida abruptamente o braço, o jovem esposo se levantou e disse:

- Por favor, senhor, eu não gostei dessa sua atitude, queira, por favor, retirar-se, pois nós ficamos magoados e constrangidos com essa sua atitude.

Ao ver e ouvir a reação do jovem esposo, os outros dois se levantaram e se dirigiram, também de forma trôpega, em direção à mesa do jovem casal.

Mesmo com todo esse movimento, o dono do restaurante só observava e mantinha-se quieto e na mesma posição de antes, em pé e com os braços escorados sobre o balcão.

- Olha aqui seu "almofadinha", disse o homem que usava um espesso bigode dirigindo-se ao jovem esposo, não nos interessa se vocês ficaram "magoadinhos" ou não e, digo mais, se nós queremos passar a mão na tua mulher, nós vamos passar a mão e ponto final, pois nada nos impedirá.

- E tem mais, "almofadinha", continuou o homem do espesso bigode, fica quieto no seu canto para não sobrar para você também, entendeu bem?

- Mas, senhor, respondeu o jovem esposo ora olhando para os três e ora olhando para o dono do restaurante, os senhores não têm o direito de nos importunar.

Com lágrimas escorrendo pelas faces, o jovem esposo continuou.

- Nós só paramos aqui para nos alimentar e descansar um pouco e já vamos seguir viagem, por favor, deixem-nos em paz que já estamos indo embora.

Falando isso, estendeu a mão para a esposa, que, prontamente, levantou-se da mesa e começaram a se dirigir ao balcão a fim de pagar a conta e se retirarem o mais rápido possível daquele ambiente que estava se tornando muito perturbador e perigoso.

Nesse mesmo momento, em movimentos que pareciam sincronizados, o homem que tinha um problema na perna foi até a porta do salão e a fechou abruptamente, o homem que tinha um corte na orelha passou os braços nos ombros e na cintura da jovem esposa e o homem do espesso bigode segurou o jovem esposo com os seus dois fortes braços.

- Não, por favor senhores, disse o casal ao mesmo tempo, permita que nós saíamos do restaurante.

- Vocês vão sair somente quando nós quisermos, disseram ao mesmo tempo os dois homens de uma maneira que parecia até uma resposta ensaiada e corriqueira para ambos.

- Por favor, a jovem esposa implorou ao dono do restaurante que assistia a cena sem se mexer, diga para esses senhores que nos deixem pagar a conta e sair.

Como o dono do restaurante continuava impassível, ela começou a chorar e suplicou aos homens que a olhavam com um estranho brilho nos olhos que a deixou em pânico:

- Por favor, eu suplico, senhores, permitam que a gente possa sair daqui.

O jovem esposo sentindo-se atordoado, também implorou:

- Por favor senhores, não nos façam mal e, se os senhores querem, eu posso dar-lhes todo o dinheiro e os cartões bancários com as senhas, que estão aqui comigo.

- Cala a boca, "almofadinha", nós não queremos o teu dinheiro, nós queremos a tua mulher, disse o homem com um corte na orelha.

- Não, por favor, não, suplicou o jovem esposo, a minha esposa está grávida e ela não pode sofrer qualquer tipo de importunação, pois isso pode prejudicar o nosso primeiro filho.

Nesse momento, o homem que tinha um problema na perna e que continuava guarnecendo a porta soltou uma sonora gargalhada no que foi imediatamente acompanhado pelos outros dois.

Mesmo com a assustadora situação, o dono do restaurante continuava impassível e não demonstrava qualquer tipo de perturbação e, muito menos, qualquer tipo de reação.

Nesse momento, o homem do espesso bigode empurrou com toda a sua força o jovem esposo para um canto do salão, o homem que tinha um corte na orelha puxava a jovem esposa e tentava beijá-la à força e o homem que tinha problema na perna continuava a rir de uma forma tão descontrolada que mais parecia o grito de uma hiena.

Como a jovem esposa caiu desmaiada no chão, o homem que a segurava abaixou-se indicando que iria se deitar no chão sobre ela.

Ao ver que a sua amada e querida jovem esposa havia desfalecido e que toda aquela situação certamente viria a prejudicar a saúde mental e emocional deles, bem como o desenvolvimento do seu tão querido e esperado filho, ele gritou do canto para onde ele havia sido atirado:

- CHEGA! CHEGA! CHEGA!

Quando ele viu que os três homens voltaram a gargalhar e que o dono do restaurante continuava impassível, ele levou a mão direita às costas e tirou da cintura uma pistola semiautomática, daquelas que carrega uma nova munição a cada disparo, e disparou, primeiro no que guarnecia a porta, depois no que lhe havia atirado no canto do salão e dando uns passos para frente também atirou no homem que estava se ajoelhando sobre a esposa e que nesse momento já havia se colocado em pé.

Os tiros foram certeiros e os três homens estavam inertes no chão, mas, mesmo assim, o jovem esposo caminhou lentamente em direção a cada um deles chamava-o de COVARDE e disparava um tiro a queima roupa na genitália e outro na têmpora de cada um deles.

Ajoelhando-se junto à jovem esposa, que apresentava estar em profundo estado de choque, pegou-a no colo, levou-a até o automóvel, beijou-a carinhosamente e disse-lhe que ela o aguardasse ali para logo seguirem com o passeio.

Ao entrar no restaurante ele foi em direção ao dono que continuava da mesma forma, impassível e debruçado sobre o balcão.

- Pois bem, perguntou o jovem esposo, o senhor viu o que aconteceu?

- Sim, vi tudo, respondeu o dono do restaurante.

- E por que o senhor não fez nada? – indagou o jovem esposo

- Eu não tinha o que fazer, e, mais a mais, o assunto não me dizia respeito, não era comigo, respondeu o dono do restaurante.

Diante dessa resposta, o jovem esposo começou a fazer-lhe várias perguntas as quais o dono do restaurante respondeu laconicamente sempre impassível e postado na mesma posição.

- O senhor já conhecia esses homens?

- Sim.

- Eles vinham seguido no seu estabelecimento?

- Sim.

- Alguma vez eles já tinham feito isso com outras mulheres?

- Sim.

- O senhor sabe se elas denunciaram o fato para as autoridades policiais?

- Não.

- O senhor os denunciou às autoridades policiais?

- Não.

- Por que o senhor não os denunciou?

- Eles eram clientes que gastavam muito no meu restaurante e, mais a mais, o assunto não me dizia respeito, respondeu irritado e demonstrando estar querendo encerrar logo ao interrogatório.

- O senhor tem esposa, tem filhos? - perguntou o jovem esposo

- Eu tenho apenas um filho e a minha esposa morreu bem jovem, respondeu o dono do restaurante.

- Pois bem, começou a falar o jovem esposo, o senhor testemunhou tudo isso e provavelmente se o senhor fosse interrogado o senhor teria condições de relatar tudo exatamente como aconteceu e, provavelmente, em um julgamento eu teria uma redução de pena por ter agido sob influência de violenta emoção.

- Mas isso não me basta, continuou o jovem esposo, eu vou ter toda a minha estragada por causa desses três doentes, que, se não fossem parados, além de continuarem soltos eu, a minha esposa e o meu filho viveríamos toda a vida atormentados com esse fato.

- Assim, continuou o jovem esposo, em vez de três seríamos seis doentes convivendo na sociedade e, agora, nesse exato momento que os três estão mortos, está nas minhas mãos, ou seja, depende da minha decisão permitir ou não que eu, a minha esposa e o meu filho tenhamos uma vida atormentada e doente até o fim dos nossos dias com a minha inevitável prisão.

- Assim, continuou o jovem esposo, se o senhor morrer e não puder testemunhar eu, a minha jovem esposa e o meu filho poderemos viver sem esse tormento de processos judiciais, condenações e prisões.

- Dessa maneira, continuou o jovem esposo, não me resta outra alternativa a não ser a de matá-lo também, mas quero lhe tranquilizar ao assumir no último momento de sua vida o compromisso de cuidar muito bem do seu filho, que não tem culpa por ter um pai omisso e conivente com violência covarde e desnecessária.

Perplexo com o que estava ouvindo, o dono do restaurante levantando os braços do balcão, retesou o corpo, arregalou os olhos e ouviu o mesmo estampido que tinha ouvido há pouco e não o tinha preocupado, já que ele pensava que aquele assunto não era com ele.

Deixando os quatro homens mortos no chão, pegou as duas garrafas de água que haviam tocado, retornou ao automóvel e perguntou para a jovem esposa:

- Estás se sentido bem?

- Sim, respondeu a jovem esposa, nós paramos nesse restaurante, fomos ao banheiro e voltamos para o automóvel, portanto agora podemos continuar o nosso passeio normalmente, meu amor.

- Ótimo, disse o esposo, então vamos seguir o nosso passeio, mas quando chegarmos na cidade eu gostaria de te levar para o hospital para que te examinem e nos digam se está tudo bem contigo e com o bebê, pode ser assim?

- Claro que pode, respondeu ela, mas me parece que isso é totalmente desnecessário.

Chegando ao hospital ele relatou que gostaria de que a esposa fosse examinada, pois, disse, ele, nós paramos em um restaurante na beira da estrada, fomos ao banheiro e comemos um sanduíche e ela não lembra que comemos o sanduíche.

Feitos todos os exames, os médicos foram unânimes em afirmar que ela estava muito bem e que, provavelmente, ela teria tido uma amnésia global transitória, que é um bastante comum de acontecer quando a pessoa está sob os efeitos de alguma emoção forte.

No dia seguinte ele disse para a esposa que não estava se sentindo muito bem e que gostaria de voltar para casa.

- Talvez aquele sanduíche que comemos naquele restaurante na beira da estrada não tenha me feito bem, disse ele.

Ela, prontamente concordou em retornar, mas brincou com ele:

- Eu é que estou grávida e tu estás tão nervoso que está sentindo efeitos de um sanduíche que nós nem comemos, completou ela com um sorriso angelical.

Chegando em casa, ele disse que precisaria ver algumas coisas no escritório e que logo voltaria.

Pegou o outro automóvel que estava na garagem e saiu em direção ao cemitério da cidade onde estava sendo enterrado o dono do restaurante.

Ao chegar viu um rapaz adolescente que estava muito abatido e que, recebia o cumprimento de todos os presentes, o que indicava ser o filho do dono do restaurante.

Encerrada a cerimônia do enterro, ele se aproximou do rapaz, expressou-lhe o sentimento de pesar pela morte do pai, e falou:

- Meu caro jovem, sou viajante e seguidamente eu parava no restaurante do seu pai e ele sempre me falava sobre você e de quanto ele te amava.

O rapaz, surpreso, olhou fixamente para aquele estranho e disse:

- Pois é, eu estou arrasado, pois eu já havia perdido a minha mãe quando era criança e agora perdi também o meu pai, estou sozinho no mundo, desabafou chorando.

- Nada disso, respondeu ele, eu vim aqui para te dizer que uma vez o teu pai me fez um grande favor e eu lhe prometi que se caso algo lhe acontecesse eu cuidaria de você e, assim, meu caro jovem, estou aqui para cumprir a me promessa e te convidando para ires até a minha casa para podermos conversar sobre o teu futuro.

Com a concordância do jovem, eles foram para a casa do jovem esposo e lá chegando, apresentou o rapaz para a esposa e disse que aquele rapaz era filho de um velho amigo que uma vez havia lhe feito um grande favor e que havia falecido e que ele gostaria que ela concordasse em tê-lo na casa deles para ajudá-lo até ele conseguir tomar conta da própria vida.

Com a concordância da esposa o rapaz passou a morar com eles e integrou-se plenamente à família deles.

Quando o agora jovem adulto estava prestes a ingressar em um curso superior ele perguntou, àquele que ele já estava chamando de pai, sobre qual seria a carreira que ele sugeriria que ele deveria seguir.

E, de pronto, o pai adotivo, respondeu:

- Creio que deves seguir a careira de direito e te especializar em crimes passionais, meu filho.

Ser e estar.

Ser eu mesmo,
sem ler,
sem falar,
sem andar,
sem beber,
sem comer,
sem meditar,
sem pensar,
sem enfeites,
sem maquiagem,
sem roupa especial,
sem semblante pesado.

Seres tu mesma,
sem ler,
sem falar,
sem andar,
sem beber,
sem comer,
sem meditar,
sem pensar,
sem enfeites,
sem maquiagem,
sem roupa especial,
sem semblante pesado.

Sermos só nós mesmos e estarmos juntos assim e
com as mãos dadas indica que
estamos nos unindo,
estamos nos amando,
estamos nos fortalecendo,
estamos nos perpetuando.

Olhares

A chefa, com um metro e noventa de altura e cento e dez quilos proporcionalmente distribuídos, caminhava com passos largos e firmes enquanto dava as ordens.

- Essa é a sua sala, senhor, entre, feche a porta, tire toda a roupa, coloque esse avental com a abertura para a frente e me aguarde.

- Essa é a sua sala, senhora, entre, feche a porta, tire toda a roupa e todas as joias, coloque esse avental com a abertura para a frente e me aguarde.

O corredor onde a chefa exercia a sua autoridade tinha várias portas nos dois lados; em um lado as salas eram identificadas por números pares e eram utilizadas para o atendimento de homens e no outro lado as salas eram identificadas por números ímpares e eram utilizadas para o atendimento de mulheres.

- Eu disse para tirar toda a roupa, senhor.

- Mas a cueca e as meias também? - perguntou o senhor de meia idade meio sem jeito.

- Sim, senhor, eu fui bem clara: é para tirar toda a roupa.

- Eu disse para tirar todas as joias, senhora.

- Mas os brincos, também? – perguntou a senhora, também de meia idade meio contrariada.

Mesmo contrariados e encabulados, ambos se despiram integralmente e colocaram o avental cinza escuro e o amarraram na frente com um cinto do mesmo pano, que estava costurado na altura da cintura.

Para mostrar que estavam prontos, ambos abriram as portas que casualmente ficavam frente a frente e ficaram se olhando por um longo tempo, mas com um olhar vago e distante como se estivessem desligados de todo o mundo ao redor.

- Me acompanhe, senhor, disse a chefa.

A chefa levou o senhor até uma porta de vidro e o entregou para o responsável pelo exame.

Em seguida a chefa, sempre caminhando firme e forte, buscou a senhora e a levou até uma grande porta de madeira e a entregou para a atendente responsável pelo exame.

Terminado o exame, a senhora voltou para a sua sala, tirou o avental e o colocou num grande cesto que era destinado às roupas utilizadas nos exames e passou a, calmamente, se vestir com suas joias e roupas.

Alguns minutos após o senhor também retornou para a sua sala, tirou o avental e o colocou num grande cesto que era destinado às roupas utilizadas nos exames e passou a tornar a se vestir rapidamente.

Como se fosse um movimento sincronizado, ambos saíram ao mesmo tempo das suas respectivas salas e se dirigiram caminhando lentamente à porta de saída percorrendo aquele longo e frio corredor.

Ao chegarem no meio do corredor onde havia uma grande janela de vidro por onde estava entrando aconchegantes raios solares, ambos pararam lado a lado e, por longo tempo, ficaram olhando para fora, mas sempre com o mesmo olhar vago e distante.

- Como te chamas? - perguntou ele.

- Ella, respondeu ela.

- E tu, como te chamas? – perguntou ela.

- Elle, respondeu ele.

- Eu gostei muito da tua companhia e eu gostaria de te ver novamente, disse Elle.

- Eu também, respondeu Ella.

- Vamos nos encontrar novamente?

- Sim, vamos.

- Onde?

- Casualmente esta semana eu passei por um bar-café no aeroporto que me causou uma forte sensação de aconchego, exatamente como a que estou sentindo agora, e que tal se nos encontrássemos lá?

- Para mim, pode ser, como se chama esse bar-café?

- Ele se chama *"Se ..."*.

- Tu vais seguidamente lá?

- Não, nunca fui, seria a minha primeira vez e como ele é grande temos que combinar um maneira de nos encontrar facilmente.

- Tens razão, que tal vestirmos sobre a nossa roupa um jaleco branco?

- Ótima ideia.

- E quando?

- Que tal na próxima quarta-feira, às dezesseis horas?

- Combinado.

Após esse diálogo, ambos continuaram caminhando com o mesmo olhar distante e vago e saíram do prédio, cada um para um lado diferente.

Naquela próxima quarta-feira, Elle chegou quando ainda faltavam cinco minutos para completar as dezesseis horas, escolheu uma mesa bem no centro do grande bar-café, sentou-se e ficou esperando Ella chegar.

Três minutos após, Ella chega no *"Se ..."* passou os olhos em todo o salão, localizou Elle e se dirigiu à mesma mesa e sentou-se.

O atento garçom dirigiu-se à mesa, deu as boas-vindas e entregou um cardápio para cada um deles.

Eles folhearam o cardápio, pediram uma xícara de chá para cada um e ficaram se olhando com o mesmo olhar vago e distante do primeiro encontro.

Após o transcurso de uma hora e com as xícaras de chá vazias, Elle perguntou.

- Podemos nos encontrar novamente?

- Sim, respondeu Ella, e por mim pode ser na próxima quarta-feira também às dezesseis horas.

- Então fica combinado, falou Elle, até a próxima quarta-feira, às dezesseis horas nessa mesma mesa.

Chamaram o garçom, pagaram as respectivas xícaras de chá, levantaram-se e saíram cada um para um lado diferente.

Aquele ritual foi realizado por tão longo tempo que quando chegava próximo das dezesseis horas de todas as quartas-feiras o garçom inclinava as duas cadeiras sobre a mesa que eles sempre ocupavam a fim de evitar que alguém eventualmente viesse a ocupá-la.

O garçom praticava o ritual da reserva mesmo não entendendo o que acontecia naquela mesa, pois os dois sempre chegavam alguns minutos antes das dezesseis horas sempre vestindo um jaleco branco, se sentavam na mesma posição da mesma mesa, pediam uma xícara do mesmo chá para cada um, ficavam em absoluto silêncio se olhando com um ar vago e distante por exatamente uma hora e saíam sem se tocar, sem falar nada e cada um sempre seguindo para um lado diferente do outro.

Em uma quarta-feira, Ella, como sempre, chegou dois minutos antes das dezesseis horas, dirigiu-se à mesma mesa e estranhou que Elle não estava lá.

Ella sentiu o seu coração começar a palpitar mais forte, sentou-se e enquanto aguardava a chegada dele a batida do seu coração ficava cada vez mais fora do controle.

Se passaram apenas dois minutos, que para Ella pareciam ter sido várias horas, quando um jovem chegou e sentou-se na outra cadeira e colocou sobre as pernas dele uma pacote que havia trazido junto.

- O meu avô me contou a história de vocês, Ella, e me pediu que eu viesse aqui e te entregasse esse pacote.

Ella, atônita, pegou o pacote, abriu-o lentamente, reconheceu o jaleco dele e olhou para o rapaz com um forte olhar indagativo e com uma voz trêmula, mas decidida, indagou:

- O que significa isso?

- O meu avô me chamou no sábado passado, me contou a história de vocês, me entregou esse pacote e me pediu que eu viesse aqui hoje para entregá-lo para a senhora.

- Sim, entendi e daí? - perguntou ela impaciente.

- O meu avô Elle faleceu no dia seguinte, no domingo, disse o rapaz com os olhos cheios de lágrimas.

Ella tomou o jaleco dele encostou-o no seu peito e começou a chorar copiosamente.

Passados quase meia hora entre momentos de choro e momentos de profunda reflexão, Ella enxugou as faces e perguntou para o rapaz:

- Podes vir aqui na próxima quarta-feira?

- Claro que posso, Ella.

Ella levantou-se e saiu levando o pacote com o jaleco de Elle em suas mãos.

Na próxima quarta-feira, o rapaz foi ao **"Se ..."**, dirigiu-se à mesma mesa alguns minutos antes das dezesseis horas, sentou-se e ficou aguardando.

Exatamente às dezesseis horas uma jovem trajando um jaleco branco sentou-se na outra cadeira com um pacote nas mãos.

- O que aconteceu? - indagou o rapaz.

- A minha avó me chamou no sábado passado, me contou a história dela e do teu avô, me entregou esse pacote com o jaleco do teu avô e me pediu que eu viesse aqui hoje para eu entregá-lo para ti.

- Sim, entendi e daí? - perguntou o rapaz.

- A minha avó Ella faleceu no dia seguinte, no domingo, disse a jovem com os olhos cheios de lágrimas.

Louco

Ela o viu sentado à mesa e dirigiu-se a ele com passos largos e firmes.

Sem ao menos cumprimentá-lo, colocou firmemente as mãos abertas sobre a mesa, inclinou o corpo para a frente, encarou-o e disparou a pergunta dura e seca:

- Tu estás louco?

- Opa, calma, o que é que houve? perguntou ele.

- Eu li o que escrevestes e volto a te perguntar: estás louco?

Ele ficou pensativo por alguns minutos até a postura dela ficar menos agressiva e falou:

- Sabes, normalmente, nenhum louco admite a loucura.

- Ele sempre acha que está certo seja no seu raciocínio, sejam nas suas palavras ou seja no seu comportamento.

- Portanto, como acho que eu estou certo, então é bem possível que eu também esteja louco.

- E tu, como te consideras? também te consideras sempre certa? perguntou ele.

Ela olhou-o fixamente, puxou uma cadeira, sentou-se à mesa e ambos ficaram em silêncio e pensando sobre a loucura e sobre o estar certo.

O som da chuva

Era madrugada.

A chuva, copiosa, a acordou.

Ela ouve o som da chuva caindo sobre o telhado e observou que ela era abundante, mas tranquila e sem vento.

Sentido que ele estava acordado ao seu lado, perguntou:

- Estás ouvindo a chuva?

- Hein? como? - indagou, ele.

Ela deslizou o corpo para mais perto ainda do corpo dele, colou os sedosos lábios no ouvido dele e repetiu, calmamente:

- Estás ouvindo a chuva?

- Não - disse ele.

- Está chovendo muito?

- Sim, muito, é uma chuva abundante, mas sem vento e tranquila - disse ela.

- Puxa, que coisa ruim ficar velho, essa deficiência auditiva me deixa triste.

- Não ouvir o cair da chuva, me deixa em estado de profunda tristeza.

- Não fique triste - disse ela.

- Eu serei os teus ouvidos e, se precisares, também os teus olhos e as tuas pernas.

- O amor que sinto por ti é muito maior que essas pequeninas deficiências.

Copiosas e abundantes lágrimas, de alegria, rolaram sobre as faces dele.

As gotículas e o oceano

- Ora, gotículas - desdenhou ele.

E, em seguida, perguntou:

- O que representam gotículas num oceano?

O outro respondeu-lhe com duas perguntas reflexivas:

- E como os oceanos são formados?

- Não são formados por gotículas?

Surpresos, um com o outro, pela pergunta do interlocutor, se afastaram e continuaram a fazer os seus distintos caminhos.

Observação

Todos os textos são frutos de uma narrativa ficcional de minha imaginação e qualquer semelhança terá sido mera coincidência.

Com exceção dos textos "O circo e a política", "Máquinas caça-níqueis" e o "Dia da mulher", que publiquei em versões reduzidas em diversos tipos de mídia, inclusive em redes sociais, todos os demais são inéditos.